SCHOLASTIC

100 LITERACY FRAMEWORK LESSONS

TERMS AND CONDITIONS

IMPORTANT - PERMITTED USE AND WARNINGS - READ CAREFULLY BEFORE USING

Licence

YEAR 3

Scottish Primary 4

Minimum specification:
- PC or Mac with a CD-ROM drive and 512 Mb RAM (recommended)
- Windows 98SE or above/Mac OSX.1 or above
- Recommended minimum processor speed: 1 GHz

For all technical support queries, please phone
Scholastic Customer Services on 0845 603 9091

Gillian Howell

CREDITS

Author
Gillian Howell

Commissioning Editor
Fiona Tomlinson

Development Editor
Simret Brar

Project Editor
Rachel Mackinnon

Assistant Editor
Victoria Lee

Series Design
Anna Oliwa &
Joy Monkhouse

Design
Sonia Bagley

Book Layout
Q2A Media

Illustrations
Jon Mitchell /
Beehive Illustration

Interactive Illustrations
Lynda Murray

CD-ROM Development
CD-ROM developed
in association with
Vivid Interactive

ACKNOWLEDGEMENTS

The publishers gratefully acknowledge permission to reproduce the following copyright material: **Nicola Bayley** for the use of an illustration from *Read and Respond: The Mousehole Cat* by Sylvia Karavis and Catherine Byrne, based on *The Mousehole Cat* by Antonia Barber. Illustration ©1998, Nicola Bayley (1998, Scholastic Ltd). **Peggy Cotton** for the use of 'Pineapple' and 'Orange' both by John Cotton from *Word whirls and other shape poems* collected by John Foster © 1998, John Cotton (1998, Oxford University Press). **John Eastwood** for the use of an illustration from *Thinderella* by Dick King-Smith, illustration © 1992, John Eastwood (1992, Victor Gollancz). **John Foster** for the use of 'The Ghost house' by John Foster from *All new 100 literacy hours: Year 3* by Gill Friel, James Friel and Sue Ellis © 2005, John Foster (2005, Scholastic Ltd). **Gill Friel** for the use of 'Beowulf and Grendel', 'A moment in time' (1), 'A moment in time'(2), 'Birds' and 'Birdwatchers' guide' all by Gill Friel from *All new 100 literacy hours: Year 3* by Gill Friel, James Friel and Sue Ellis © 2005, Gill Friel (2005, Scholastic Ltd). **James Friel** for the use of 'Dinosaurs – when and where' and 'Dinosaurs – sizes and shapes' both by James Friel from *All new 100 literacy hours: Year 3* by Gill Friel, James Friel and Sue Ellis © 2005, James Friel (2005, Scholastic Ltd). **Her Majesty's Stationery Office** for the use of extracts and an illustration from 'Rules for Pedestrians: Crossing the road 7 a., b., c., d., and e' from the website www.highwaycode.gov.uk/01.htm © Crown copyright, reproduced under the terms of the Click-Use Licence. Use of Crown copyright material is reproduced with the permission of the Controller of HMSO and the Queen's Printer for Scotland. **Her Majesty's Stationery Office** for the use of the hedgehog illustrations for The Green Cross Code taken from http://www.hedgehogs.gov.uk/morehh/wallpapers/wallpaper_1_800.jpg © Crown copyright material is reproduced with the permission of the Controller of HMSO and the Queen's Printer for Scotland (HMSO Licence V2006000828). **David Higham Associates** for the use of a text extract and an illustration from *Don't put your finger in the jelly, Nelly* by Nick Sharratt, text and illustration © 1993, Nick Sharratt (1993, Hippo Books). **David Higham Associates** for the use of an extract from *Midnight for Charlie Bone* by Jenny Nimmo © 2002, Jenny Nimmo (2002, Egmont). **Hodder and Stoughton Ltd** for the use of a text extract and an illustration from *Red eyes at night* by Michael Morpurgo. Text © 1998, Michael Morpurgo. Illustration © 1998, Tony Ross (1998, Hodder Children's Books). **Libby Houston** for the use of 'Black dot' by Libby Houston from *All Change* by Libby Houston © 1974; 1993, Libby Houston (1993, Oxford University Press). **Tony Langham** for the use of 'Autumn' by Tony Langham from *Word whirls and other shape poems* collected by John Foster © 1998, Tony Langham (1998, Oxford University Press). **Frances Lincoln Ltd** for the use of text and illustrations from *The colour of home* by Mary Hoffman. Text © 2002, Mary Hoffman Illustration © 2002, Karin Littlewood (2002, Frances Lincoln Ltd). **The Peters Fraser and Dunlop Group Ltd** for the use of 'An attempt at unrhymed verse' from *The Orchard Book of Funny Poems* by Wendy Cope © 1996, Wendy Cope (1996, Orchard Books). **Gervase Phinn** for the use of 'Holiday Memories' by Paula Edwards from *Lizard over Ice* edited by Gervase Phinn © 1990, Paula Edwards (1990, Nelson Thornes). **The Random House Group** for the use of an extract from *Timid Tim and the Cuggy Thief* by John Prater © 1994, John Prater (1994, Red Fox). **John Rice** for the use of 'Conversation at the school dinner table' by John Rice from *Zoomballoomballistic* by John Rice © 1982, John Rice (1982, Aten Press). **Walker Books Ltd** for the use of an extract from *The Mousehole Cat* by Antonia Barber, illustrated by Nicola Bayley © 1990, Antonia Barber (1990, Walker Books Ltd). **A.P. Watt Ltd** on behalf of Fox Busters Ltd and Dick King-Smith for the use of text from *A mouse called Wolf* by Dick King-Smith © 1997, Fox Busters Ltd (1997, Transworld Publishers Ltd); an extract from 'Taken away' by Dick King-Smith from *Daggie Dogfoot* by Dick King-Smith © 1980, Dick King-Smith (1980, Victor Gollancz); 'Little Miss Muffet', 'Georgie Porgie' and 'Hickory Dickory Dock' by Dick King-Smith from *The Topsy-Turvy Storybook* by Dick King-Smith © 1992, Foxbusters Ltd (1992, Victor Gollancz). **David Whitehead** for the use of 'Rainbow' by David Whitehead from *Scholastic Collections: Poetry* compiled by Wes Magee © 1992, David Whitehead (1992, Scholastic Ltd). **Kit Wright** for the use of 'Heads or tails?' by Kit Wright from *Hot dog and other poems* by Kit Wright © 1981, Kit Wright (1981, Kestrel Books).

Every effort has been made to trace copyright holders for the works reproduced in this book, and the publishers apologise for any inadvertent omissions.

Post-it is a registered trademark of 3M.

Text © 2007, Gillian Howell
© 2007 Scholastic Ltd

Designed using Adobe InDesign

Published by Scholastic Ltd
Villiers House
Clarendon Avenue
Leamington Spa
Warwickshire CV32 5PR

Visit our website at
www.scholastic.co.uk

Printed by Bell and Bain Ltd
456789 890123456

British Library Cataloguing-in-Publication Data
A catalogue record for this book is available from the British Library.
ISBN 978-0439-94523-3

CONTENTS

Introduction	**3**
Checklists	6
Narrative	**9**
Unit 1	9
Unit 2	25
Unit 3	45
Unit 4	65
Unit 5	83
Non-fiction	**101**
Unit 1	101
Unit 2	121
Unit 3	137
Poetry	**157**
Unit 1	157
Unit 2	168
Unit 3	181

INTRODUCTION
100 Literacy Framework Lessons: Year 3

About the series

The *100 Literacy Framework Lessons* series is a response to the Primary National Strategy's revised Literacy Framework and contains **all new** material. The lessons mirror the structure and learning objectives of the Exemplification Units of the Framework. The CD-ROM provides appropriate and exciting texts and also contains a variety of other resources from videos and images to audio and weblinks, which will help to guide you in implementing the Framework's emphasis on ICT texts. The books and CD-ROMs will be an invaluable resource to help you understand and implement the revised Framework.
The key points of the revised framework are:

- The development of early reading and phonics;
- Coherent and progressive teaching of word-level and sentence-level embedded into learning or taught discretely;
- Following and building upon the teaching sequence from reading to writing and developing comprehension;
- Flexible lessons providing a challenging pace;
- Integration of speaking and listening skills;
- Planning for inclusion;
- Broadening and strengthening pedagogy.

Early reading and phonics

The authors of the *100 Literacy Framework Lessons* have endeavoured to incorporate all of the above with one exception, the teaching of phonics. The Government is advising that phonics is taught using a systematic, discrete and time-limited programme. However, where possible we have made links to phonic focuses that you might want to identify when teaching the lesson.

It is important to note that the renewed Framework is advocating a change from the Searchlight model of teaching early reading to the 'simple view of reading', *"The knowledge and skills within the four Searchlight strategies are subsumed within the two dimensions of word recognition and language comprehension of the 'two simple views of reading'. For beginner readers, priority should be given to securing word recognition, knowledge and skills"* (from the PNS Core Papers document). Phonic work will be time limited and as children develop their early reading skills they will then move from learning to read to learning to learn.

Quest myth map

Using the book
The book is divided into three parts, called Blocks: Narrative Block, Non-fiction Block and Poetry Block. This reflects the structure of the renewed Framework planning. The Blocks are divided into Units, each Unit covers a different text-type within the Block, for example in the Narrative Block there might be one Unit which covers 'myths and legends' and another that covers 'plays'. Units are taught on a specified amount of weeks and are split into Phases. Phases vary in length and are essentially a way to focus on a specific part of teaching relating to the Unit. Phases are then divided into days, or lessons, which then contain the teaching activities. Unlike the *100 All New Literacy Hours,* this book has not been divided into terms because one of the main points of the Framework is flexibility and this structure will let teachers adapt to their particular children's needs.

Block [genres] ➤ Units [text-type] ➤ Phases [section of Unit] ➤ Days/Lessons [Individual lessons]

Units
Each Unit covers a different text-type, or genre and because of this each Unit has its own introduction containing the following:
Objectives: All objectives for the Unit are listed under their strand names.
Progression: Statements about the progression that the children should make within the Unit's focus, for example narrative text-type.
Aspects of learning: Key aspects of learning that the Unit covers.
Prior learning: Key elements that the children need to be able to do before they commence the lessons.
Cross-curricular opportunities: Integrating other areas of the curriculum into the literacy lessons.
Resources: Everything required for the lesson that teachers may not have readily available.
Teaching sequence: This is an overview chart of the Unit. It shows the number of Phases, children's objectives, a summary of activities and the learning outcomes.

Unit lesson plans
The lesson plans all follow the same format. There are three columns and each contains different information.
Key features: The key features column provides an at-a-glance view of the key aspects of learning covered in the lesson.
Stages: The stages column provides the main lesson plans.
Additional opportunities: This column provides additional opportunities for the lesson. This is where there will be links made to phonics, high frequency words, support or extension activities and any other relevant learning opportunities.

End of Phase

At the end of each Phase there are three boxes containing Guided reading or writing ideas, Assessment ideas and Further work.

Guided: The guided box contains ideas for guided reading or writing. These have been included separately as there seems to be a trend to do this work outside of the literacy hour lesson. These ideas can either be integrated into a lesson or taught at a separate time.

Assessment: There are two types of assessment.

End of Phase assessments: These are mainly observations of the children or simple tasks to see whether they have understood what has been taught in the Phase. Teachers are referred back to the learning outcomes in the teaching sequence in the Unit introduction.

End of Unit assessments: These are activities which range from interactive activities, to working from a stimulus image, to completing a photocopiable sheet. They can be found on the CD-ROM accompanying this series.

Further work: Further work provides opportunities for the teacher to extend or support the children following the assessment activity.

Photocopiable pages

At the end of each Unit are the photocopiable pages. These can also be found on the CD-ROM.

Using the CD-ROM

This is a basic guide for using the CD-ROM; for more detailed information please go to 'How to use the CD-ROM' on the start-up screen of the CD-ROM.

The CD-ROM contains resources for each book in the series. These might include: text extracts, differentiated text extracts, editable text extracts, photocopiable pages, interactive activities, images, videos, audio files, PowerPoint files, weblinks and assessment activities. There are also skeleton frames based on Sue Palmer's skeletons for teaching non-fiction text types. Also on the CD-ROM are the lesson notes for easy planning as Word file documents.

You can access resources in a number of ways:

Phase menu: The Phase menu provides all the resources used in that Phase. There are tabs at the top of the page denoting the resource type, for example 'Text'. If you click on this tab you will see a series of buttons to your left; if you press these then you will be taken to the other texts used within that Phase. You can print two versions of the text: either the screen – which shows any annotations made (see Whiteboard tools below) or Print PDF version, which will print an A4 size.

Resources menu: The resource menu lists every resource that is available on the CD-ROM. You can search by type of resource.

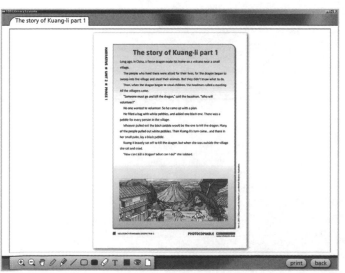

Whiteboard tools: This series contains a set of whiteboard tools. These can be used with any interactive whiteboard and from a computer connected to a projector. The tools available are: Hand tool – so that when you zoom in you can move around the screen; Zoom in; Zoom out; Pen tool for freehand writing or drawing; Highlighter; Line tool; Box tool; Text tool; Eraser tool; Clear screen; Hide annotations; Colour. You cannot save any changes made to the texts so always remember to 'Print Screen' when you annotate the CD-ROM pages.

Speak and listen for a range of purposes on paper and on screen strand checklist

	Narrative Unit 1	Narrative Unit 2	Narrative Unit 3	Narrative Unit 4	Narrative Unit 5	Non-fiction Unit 1	Non-fiction Unit 2	Non-fiction Unit 3	Poetry Unit 1	Poetry Unit 2	Poetry Unit 3
Strand 1 Speaking											
Choose and prepare poems or stories for performance, identifying appropriate expression, tone, volume and use of voices and other sounds.									✔		✔
Explain process or present information, ensuring items are clearly sequenced, relevant details are included and accounts ended effectively.						✔	✔	✔			
Sustain conversation, explain or give reasons for their views or choices.	✔			✔	✔					✔	✔
Develop and use specific vocabulary in different contexts.											
Strand 2 Listening and responding											
Follow up others' points and show whether they agree or disagree in whole-class discussion.	✔										
Identify the presentational features used to communicate the main points in a broadcast.						✔					
Identify key sections of an informative broadcast, noting how the language used signals changes or transitions in focus.						✔					
Strand 3 Group discussion and interaction											
Use discussion to organise roles and action.		✔		✔	✔	✔	✔				
Actively include and respond to all members of the group.		✔		✔		✔	✔		✔		
Use the language of possibility to investigate and reflect on feelings, behaviour or relationships.			✔		✔						
Strand 4 Drama											
Present events and characters through dialogue to engage the interest of an audience.					✔						
Use some drama strategies to explore stories or issues.	✔		✔		✔						
Identify and discuss qualities of others' performances, including gesture, action and costume.					✔				✔		

Read for a range of purposes on paper and on screen strand checklist

	Narrative Unit 1	Narrative Unit 2	Narrative Unit 3	Narrative Unit 4	Narrative Unit 5	Non-fiction Unit 1	Non-fiction Unit 2	Non-fiction Unit 3	Poetry Unit 1	Poetry Unit 2	Poetry Unit 3
Strand 5 Word recognition											
Objectives covered by the end of Year 2.											
Strand 6 Word structure and spelling											
Spell high and medium frequency words.									✔		✔
Recognise a range of prefixes and suffixes, understanding how they modify meaning and spelling and how they assist in decoding long, complex words.											✔
Spell unfamiliar words using known conventions including phoneme/grapheme correspondences and morphological rules.						✔					✔
Strand 7 Understanding and interpreting texts											
Identify and make notes on the main points of section(s) of text.						✔					
Infer characters' feelings in fiction and consequences in logical explanations.			✔	✔							
Identify how different texts are organised, including reference texts, magazines and leaflets, on paper and on screen.						✔	✔	✔			
Use syntax, context and word structure to build their store of vocabulary when reading for meaning.											
Explore how different texts appeal to readers using varied sentence structures and descriptive language.	✔		✔	✔					✔	✔	✔
Strand 8 Engaging with and responding to texts											
Share and compare reasons for reading preferences, extending range of books read.	✔		✔	✔	✔						
Empathise with characters and debate moral dilemmas portrayed in texts.			✔		✔						
Identify features that writers use to provoke readers' reactions.	✔	✔	✔	✔	✔	✔		✔	✔	✔	✔

Write for a range of purposes on paper and on screen strand checklist

	Narrative Unit 1	Narrative Unit 2	Narrative Unit 3	Narrative Unit 4	Narrative Unit 5	Non-fiction Unit 1	Non-fiction Unit 2	Non-fiction Unit 3	Poetry Unit 1	Poetry Unit 2	Poetry Unit 3
Strand 9 Creating and shaping texts											
Make decisions about form and purpose, identify success criteria and use them to evaluate their own writing.			✔		✔	✔	✔				✔
Use beginning, middle and end to write narratives in which events are sequenced logically and conflicts resolved.		✔	✔								
Write non-narrative texts using structures of different text-types.						✔		✔			
Select and use a range of technical and descriptive vocabulary.	✔		✔		✔	✔	✔	✔		✔	
Use layout, format, graphics amd illustrations for different purposes.				✔	✔	✔	✔	✔		✔	✔
Strand 10 Text structure and organisation											
Signal sequence, place and time to give coherence.		✔	✔		✔	✔	✔	✔	✔		
Group related material into paragraphs.			✔	✔		✔	✔	✔			
Strand 11 Sentence structure and punctuation											
Show relationships of time, reason and cause, through subordination and connectives.		✔	✔		✔	✔	✔	✔	✔		
Compose sentences using adjectives, verbs and nouns for precision, clarity and impact.	✔		✔	✔	✔	✔	✔	✔		✔	✔
Clarify meaning through the use of exclamation marks and speech marks.			✔			✔					
Strand 12 Presentation											
Write with consistency in size and proportion of letters and spacing within and between words, using the correct formation of handwriting joins.	✔		✔	✔	✔	✔	✔		✔	✔	✔
Develop accuracy and speed when using keyboard skills to type, edit and re-draft.	✔			✔	✔		✔	✔	✔	✔	✔

NARRATIVE
UNIT 1 Stories with familiar settings

Speak and listen for a range of purposes on paper and on screen

Strand 1 Speaking
■ Sustain conversation, explain or give reasons for their views or choices.
Strand 2 Listening and responding
■ Follow up others' points and show whether they agree or disagree in whole-class discussion.
Strand 4 Drama
■ Use some drama strategies to explore stories or issues.

Read for a range of purposes on paper and on screen

Strand 7 Understanding and interpreting texts
■ Explore how different texts appeal to readers using varied sentence structures and descriptive language.
Strand 8 Engaging and responding to texts
■ Share and compare reasons for reading preferences, extending range of books read.
■ Identify features that writers use to provoke readers' reactions.

Write for a range of purposes on paper and on screen

Strand 9 Creating and shaping texts
■ Select and use a range of technical and descriptive vocabulary.
Strand 11 Sentence structure and punctuation
■ Compose sentences using adjectives, verbs and nouns for precision, clarity and impact.
Strand 12 Presentation
■ Write with consistency in size and proportion of letters and spacing within and between words, using the correct formation of handwriting joins.
■ Develop accuracy and speed when using keyboard skills to type, edit and re-draft.

Progression in narrative

In this year children are moving towards:
■ Consolidating understanding of sequential story structure: identifying common, formal elements in story openings and endings and typical features of particular types of story; noticing common themes, similar key incidents and typical phrases or expressions.
■ Making deductions about characters' feelings, behaviour and relationships based on descriptions and their actions in the story; making judgements about a character's actions, demonstrating empathy.
■ Exploring settings used to create atmosphere.

UNIT 1 ◀ Stories with familiar settings continued

Key aspects of learning covered in this Unit

Reasoning
Children will ask questions about the reasons for events in stories, returning to the text for evidence and applying their wider knowledge and experience.

Information processing
Children will identify relevant information from different texts on paper and on screen and will use these to support their own writing.

Evaluation
Children will discuss criteria for their written work, give feedback to others and judge the effectiveness of their own descriptions.

Empathy
Writing and listening to stories based on first-hand experience will help children to understand what others might be thinking or feeling in a particular situation.

Social skills
When working collaboratively, children will listen to and respect other people's ideas. They will undertake a variety of roles in group contexts.

Communication
Children will develop their ability to discuss as they work collaboratively in paired, group and whole-class contexts. They will communicate outcomes orally, in writing and through ICT if appropriate.

Prior learning

Before starting this Unit check that the children can:
■ Identify the elements of a familiar setting when discussing a story read on paper and on screen.
■ Compose and punctuate a simple sentence.
If they need further support please refer to a prior Unit or a similar Unit in Year 2.

Resources

Phase 1:
The Julian Stories: A Pudding like a Night on the Sea by Ann Cameron, or another story with a familiar setting; *The colour of home extracts 1 and 2* by Mary Hoffman 🎨 and the complete book, if possible; *The Mousehole Cat* by Antonia Barber 🎨; Photocopiable page 22 'Venn diagram'; Photocopiable page 23 'Settings'; Photocopiable page 24 'Senses'; Zones of relevance board 🎨

Phase 2:
The colour of home extracts 1 and 2 by Mary Hoffman 🎨; *The Julian Stories: A Pudding like a Night on the Sea* by Ann Cameron or another story with a familiar setting; *The Mousehole Cat* by Antonia Barber 🎨

Phase 3:
Pictures of familiar settings from magazines, newspapers and so on; Digital photographs of familiar settings from the local area; Digital camera and photo editing software; Slideshow software; Photocopiable page 23 'Settings'; Stimulus images: harbour, woodland, playground, shopping centre, busy street 🎨

Cross-curricular opportunities

Geography – the local area
Art and Design

UNIT 1 ■ Teaching sequence

Phase	Children's objectives	Summary of activities	Learning outcomes
1	I can listen and respond.	Introduce the class story; discuss characters and settings; write a sentence.	Children can express views clearly as part of a group discussion.
		Introduce a second story; compare and contrast settings on a chart.	
	I can discuss and draw comparisons.	Hot-seat children as a character from the story; use the senses to describe settings.	Children can form opinions of a text and use evidence.
	I can read and respond.	Introduce a story with a different setting. Identify viewpoint. Draw up a list of settings to use in independent writing.	
2	I can analyse language.	Identify main impressions of a setting, group role play miming the atmosphere.	Children can express views clearly as part of a group discussion.
	I can choose alternative vocabulary.	Describe a setting, changing the atmosphere. Collaborate in writing sentences.	Children can form opinions of a text and use evidence in the text to explain their reasons.
	I can create a problem for a character.	Plan and write a first event for a story. Group discussion of problems for the plot.	Children can use visual elements to write sentences describing settings.
	I can take ownership of writing.	Continue the class story, adding a problem and resolution. Children change the class story independently.	
3	I can explore images.	Explore pictures of a variety of familiar settings. Role play exploring a setting.	Children can compose and punctuate a series of sentences to describe a familiar setting.
	I can create success criteria.	Explore digital photos of settings. Collect vocabulary. Discuss success criteria.	
	I can write an opening sentence.	Identify language to create atmosphere. Improve a sentence.	
	I can make notes.	Collect imaginative vocabulary and write a first draft.	
	I can write a setting description.	Edit, improve and complete setting descriptions.	
	I can use images to enhance writing.	Explore images on computer. Manipulate images to enhance written work.	
	I can contribute to a class presentation.	Create a class slideshow presentation.	

Provide copies of the objectives for the children.

DAY 1 ■ Listen and respond to stories

Key features	Stages	Additional opportunities
Reasoning: return to the text for evidence to support their ideas	**Introduction** Read the story *A Pudding like a Night on the Sea* from *The Julian Stories*, or another story with a familiar setting to the class. Ask the children to describe what the story is about. Encourage them to describe the setting. Ask them to suggest words and phrases from the story that told them about the setting.	**MFW:** something, thought
Social skills: collaborate with a partner	**Speaking and listening** Ask the children to think about the characters in the story. Create a chart of the three main characters: father, Huey and Julian, and ask the children to discuss with a partner what each character is like. Ask them to come and add words and phrases to the chart that describe their actions, appearances and personalities. Focus on a description of a character, such as Father on pages 9–11 of *The Julian Stories*. Ask the children for words and phrases to describe the story's atmosphere. Use the Zones of relevance board from the CD-ROM to group their suggestions. Keep a copy for the next lesson.	**Support:** revise adjectives to describe appearance and personality **Extend:** encourage the use of imaginative vocabulary
	Independent work Ask the children to write a sentence to describe the setting of the story, and a sentence describing the atmosphere.	**Extend:** discuss imagery, literal and figurative
	Plenary Read some of the sentences. Discuss and compare similarities and differences in their opinions.	

DAY 2 ■ Comparing settings

Key features	Stages	Additional opportunities
Reasoning: return to the text for evidence to support their ideas	**Introduction** Remind the children about the characters and setting from the story they read yesterday. Ask them what they feel about the main character's home. *Is it happy, warm, lively, fun, exciting? Why?*	**MFW:** without, outside, father, mother, sister, grandparents, uncle, cousins
Empathy: understand how others might be feeling	**Speaking and listening** Refer to the Zones of relevance board from yesterday's session. Ask children to add further descriptive words or phrases about how they feel about Julian's home. Display *The colour of home extract 1* from the CD-ROM Read the description and talk about the setting. Ask how all the colours make them feel about the setting. Discuss what is similar and different about Hassan and Julian's homes. Display extract 2. Ask if the second part of the description has changed the way they feel. Ask them to suggest words or phrases to describe the setting now. Display photocopiable page 22 'Venn diagram' and model how to write words or phrases on the diagram to compare the setting of the story from Day 1 and *The colour of home*.	**Support:** revise colour words **Extend:** use adventurous vocabulary and express feelings
	Independent work Ask the children to work with a partner and write their own words and phrases to compare both settings using the photocopiable sheet.	
	Plenary Read *The colour of home* by Mary Hoffman to the children.	

DAY 3 ■ Using the senses to describe settings

Key features	Stages	Additional opportunities
Reasoning: reasons for events	**Introduction** Remind the children of the story read in yesterday's plenary. Ask the children to retell what they remember about the story. At this point you might like to re-read the story to the children. Ask them to suggest why the author chose the title.	
Empathy: understand how others might be feeling **Self-awareness:** role play	**Speaking and listening** Invite the children to imagine Hassan is a new boy in their class. Discuss what they would like to ask him. Encourage them to think about the changes in what Hassan sees, smells and hears, and his feelings. Choose some children to sit in the hot-seat in the role of Hassan, and encourage the others to ask him questions.	**Support:** provide children with a list of question words for asking open-ended questions
Communication: work collaboratively	**Independent work** Ask the children to work with a partner and choose either the story from Day 1 or *The colour of home*. Tell them to think about the setting of their chosen story and, together, draw up a list of what they might see, hear and smell in the setting. Gather the children together again and collect and compare their ideas about each of the two settings.	**Support:** use photocopiable page 23 'Settings' to give children examples as a stimulus
	Plenary Ask the children which setting they prefer and why. Ask how important they think the senses are in a setting description. *What other senses could also be used?*	

DAY 4 ■ The senses and settings

Key features	Stages	Additional opportunities
	Introduction Discuss with the children how all stories have certain things in common – characters, settings and a series of events with a problem to solve. Tell them they are going to start working on their own setting descriptions. Ask the children to say which of the two stories that they have read so far appealed most to them and why. Ask: *What created the atmosphere in the story from Day 1?* Repeat the question for *The colour of home*.	**MFW:** terrible, indoors, friendly, strength, giant
Information processing: identify relevant information	**Speaking and listening** Display *The Mousehole Cat* from the CD-ROM and read it together. Ask them to tell you their first impressions about the setting and the atmosphere. Ask which senses have been used in the description (sight and sound) and use two colours with the Highlighter tool to identify sight and sound words and phrases on the text. Together, draw up a list of settings the children are most familiar with in their own lives, such as home, school, playground.	**Extend:** explain why they empathise with characters, events or setting **Support:** explain metaphor and simile and find examples in the text
Communication: collaborate with others	**Independent work** Ask the children to work with a partner and choose a setting from the list. Tell them to discuss the setting and make a list of what they might see, feel, smell, and hear.	**Support:** use photocopiable page 23 'Settings' to stimulate ideas
	Plenary Ask some of the children to read their lists without saying what the setting is. Ask others to guess the setting from the list of sights, sounds and so on.	

Guided reading

Select an appropriate text or read *Because of Figs* from *The Julian Stories*. Ask the children to identify sentences and point out the punctuation. Discuss the use of paragraphs and ask the children to say how they are linked Focus on the setting and ask the children to identify where senses have been used to add descriptions about the setting. Invite them to say which senses are used and to picture the scene in their heads.

Assessment

Provide each group of children with a copy of photocopiable page 24 'Senses'.

Choose one child to scribe for the group. Ask them to discuss the illustration of the setting and make notes of the group's ideas about it beneath each heading.

Does each member make contributions? Is the group able to accept and build on each other's suggestions?

Refer back to the learning outcomes on page 11.

Further work

Provide the children with a range of stories with familiar settings. Ask them to identify the setting for each of the stories. Ask them to use their senses to describe the setting.

Ask the children to re-read *A Pudding Like a Night on the Sea* and *The colour of home* and make a note any senses used during the stories.

DAY 1 ■ Language used to create atmosphere

Key features	Stages	Additional opportunities
	Introduction Remind the children of the two stories they read in the previous Phase. Ask them to retell the story they most enjoyed and say why they preferred it. Explain that you are going to read the two extracts once more together and think about the main impression they give readers about the setting.	
	Speaking and listening Ask the children to work with a partner and to discuss and compare each other's main impressions. Ask them to find the key words that led to this impression. Take feedback from the class. Now focus on *The Mousehole Cat*. Ask the children if they think the atmosphere is calm, threatening, angry or peaceful. Display the text from the CD-ROM and highlight the words and phrases that give a) a threatening feeling and b) a calm feeling, using different colours.	**Support:** ask the children to find angry or threatening verbs and calm adjectives
Social skills: collaborate with others; take up a role	**Independent work** Ask the children to work with a partner and plan a short mime of this scene from *The Mousehole Cat*. One child takes the role of The Great Storm Cat and the other the role of Mowzer. Ask volunteers to perform their mimes for the other children.	
	Plenary Ask the children to say two things they really liked about the mimes. How do the children show the difference between The Great Storm Cat and Mowzer?	

DAY 2 ■ Changing the atmosphere of settings

Key features	Stages	Additional opportunities
Information processing: identify relevant information	**Introduction** Ask the children to turn to a partner and say one word to describe The Great Storm Cat. Discuss their responses. Tell the children that in this session you are going to think about how to change the atmosphere of the setting from threatening to calm and peaceful. Explain that the author has used The Great Storm Cat as a metaphor for the wind. Ask the children to recall what The Great Storm Cat did to create atmosphere, for example *howled*, *clawed*. Ask them to suggest what it would do when the setting was peaceful, for example *sleep, rest, purr, stretch*. Display the text from the CD-ROM and read the second paragraph to the children. Ask for suggestions of what Mowzer would see and hear if the setting was calm. Draw up a list of nouns and verbs from their suggestions.	**Support:** explain metaphor and simile
Social skills: listen to other people's ideas	**Speaking and listening** Ask the children to imagine they are looking at the scene from a window. What can they see and hear? How do they feel? Tell them to describe the scene to a partner. On the board, model writing an opening sentence for a peaceful atmosphere in the setting. Ask the children for suggestions for a second sentence. Change word order, delete or add other words until the children find the best sentence. Keep a copy for the next day.	**Support:** ask the children to close their eyes and picture the scene in their heads **Extend:** suggest suitable adjectives and adverbs to enhance the setting
	Plenary Discuss other books they are reading with calm settings. Ask them to say why these settings seem peaceful.	

DAY 3 ■ Creating events for the setting

Key features	Stages	Additional opportunities
Evaluation: judge the effectiveness of what has been written so far	**Introduction** Read the sentences that were created to describe a peaceful setting in the previous session. Ask the children to suggest further improvements. Explain that, together, you are going to plan and write an episode for a story that begins in this setting. Remind the children of the main ingredients for story writing. They have the setting – a peaceful harbour – and tell them the main character is a dog called Charlie. Ask them to think of a first event and discuss their suggestions.	**Extend:** encourage children to think how they can keep the atmosphere they have established so far
Social skills: work collaboratively	**Speaking and listening** Ask them to picture the setting in their heads, then to work with a partner and discuss an event. It might be something Charlie sees happening, or does himself. Tell them to take five minutes to discuss their ideas with a partner. Gather them together and take feedback. Collaborate with them in writing one or two sentences to continue the story, altering and improving vocabulary and checking punctuation and spelling. Keep a copy for future use.	**Support:** remind the children of key story ingredients: opening, build up, problem, complication, resolution
	Independent work Ask children in small groups to discuss what is needed to move the story along. Encourage each group to decide on a problem for Charlie to solve, and write them down.	
	Plenary Take feedback from the groups of their problem ideas.	

DAY 4 ■ Problems and solutions

Key features	Stages	Additional opportunities
	Introduction Ask the children to read the story so far. Explain that this is a collaborative story, and each child as a writer would have their own individual ideas.	
	Speaking and listening Encourage them to talk with a partner about how they would change the story to make it their own. Take feedback.	
Evaluation: discuss criteria, give feedback and judge effectiveness	**Independent work** Ask them to take ten minutes to write the story with a partner, up to the point where the collaborative story finishes, and make any changes to the setting and events that they wish.	**Support:** write the story without adding their own changes
Reasoning: reasons for events in stories	**Whole-class work** Gather the children together and remind them of some of the problems they had thought about at the end of the previous session. Write some of their problem-suggestions on the board, and discuss with them how these might be solved and the story concluded. Choose one problem and solution and model how to add them to the story.	**Extend:** ask the children to write their own problems and resolutions independently
	Plenary Read the story aloud. Discuss what works well and what could be improved. Ask them to vote on the outcome. *Is this a good story?* Ask them to support their opinions with reasons.	

Guided reading

Select an appropriate text at the right level for the group. Focus on setting description and ask them to identify descriptive language, adjectives, adverbs and comparisons (similes). Ask the children to suggest what the mood of the setting is and find words and phrases that support their opinion.

Discuss the use of paragraphs and ask the children to say how they are linked.

Identify any speech punctuation and ask children to show how it opens and closes dialogue.

Assessment

Observation: Are the children able to identify vocabulary that is used to affect the atmosphere in the texts? Are they able to vary their sentences to create an atmosphere?

Do the children use capital letters and full stops?

Refer back to the learning outcomes on page 11.

Further work

Provide a selection of stories and ask the children to group them according to the mood or atmosphere of the settings.

Ask the children to collect words and phrases that indicate the mood of a story in their reading diaries.

Give the children a complex or compound sentence and ask them to change it into simple sentences using correct punctuation.

DAY 1 ■ Exploring images

Key features	Stages	Additional opportunities
	Introduction Explain that the children are going to be exploring a variety of settings and working towards writing their own setting descriptions. Remind them about how they used the senses to describe settings in the previous sessions, and how these helped to create an atmosphere. Ask the children for suggestions of different atmospheres or feelings that settings could evoke, for example lonely and frightening, happy, busy and bustling.	**Support:** use a thesaurus to find alternative vocabulary
Social skills: listen and respond to others' ideas; group role play	**Speaking and listening** Provide each group of children with several pictures of different familiar settings from magazines and newspapers. Ask the groups to look closely at the pictures and discuss what the settings are. Tell each group to choose one setting that they agree they would like to explore. Ask them to discuss what they would do in the setting, and what they would see and hear. Ask the groups to role play their setting without using their voices. Tell them to use gestures and facial expressions to demonstrate what they are doing and how they feel – what the atmosphere is. Gather the class together again and write headings of the settings chosen by the groups. Add vocabulary to each heading to show what they saw and heard, and how they were feeling.	**Word bank:** collect vocabulary relating to the senses and add to personal word banks
Empathy: understand how others might be feeling	**Plenary** Ask some of the groups to demonstrate their role play to the other children. Ask the audience to say what they think the group members are feeling.	

DAY 2 ■ Digital images

Key features	Stages	Additional opportunities
Communication: communicate orally in whole-class contexts	**Introduction** Display digital photographs of local familiar settings, taken prior to the session. Include some taken from unusual angles or directions. Explain that these are images of settings the children might be very familiar with. Tell them that you are going to explore the settings in detail and generate ideas for creating different atmospheres. Explore the images one at a time, asking the children to describe the setting. Encourage the children to suggest how these settings make them feel. What sort of atmosphere do they have? Collect the children's suggestions as vocabulary to use in later writing. Focus on different parts of the image and ask children to suggest adjectives to describe what they see. If possible, use a spotlight tool to isolate parts of the photograph and add vocabulary to the spotlight from the children's suggestions. Keep a copy.	**Extend:** use a digital camera to take photographs of settings in the school area to experiment with manipulating images using photo processing software
Social skills: collaborate with a partner	**Speaking and listening** Remind the children of the work they have done on settings in previous sessions. Ask them to work with a partner and discuss the ingredients needed to write effective sentences to describe a setting.	
	Independent work Working individually, ask the children to write their personal list of ingredients for achieving success in describing settings.	**Support:** provide children with photocopiable page 23 'Settings'
	Plenary Read and compare the success criteria.	

DAY 3 ▪ A first draft

Key features	Stages	Additional opportunities
Reasoning: ask questions, refer to evidence	**Introduction** Explain that, together, you are going to use one of the images from the previous sessions as a stimulus for writing a description of the setting, as if it were the opening of a story. Re-visit some of the memorable images from the magazines and photographs and together choose one to work with. Display the image and the notes from the class contributions made during the previous sessions under the setting headings and/or with a spotlight tool. Talk through the suggestions, focusing on descriptive language, such as adjectives and adverbs, and ask the children which ones they feel are the most effective. Remind them of the work they did on describing atmosphere. Ask the children to suggest what the mood of the setting should be, for example a frightening forest. Highlight or delete words and phrases from the children's input. Model how to write an opening sentence, checking spelling and punctuation with the class. Ask the children to suggest the next few sentences and scribe them on the board. Keep a copy.	**Extend:** encourage children to suggest more powerful and interesting adjectives **Extend:** ask the children to write the sentences on the board
Social skills and communication: collaborate with a partner, listen and respond	**Independent work** Ask the children to work with a partner and read the first draft on the board to each other, orally adding to or deleting from to improve it. Ask them to write their improved version together.	
	Plenary Read some of the children's improvements and discuss which ones work best and why.	

DAY 4 ▪ Making notes

Key features	Stages	Additional opportunities
	Introduction Display the first draft written yesterday. Using some of the children's improved versions, model how to edit the draft to improve it. Focus on the sentence structures and punctuation. Demonstrate how to alter the order of sentences, phrases and clauses to change the effect. Discuss how altering the sentences can have an effect on the punctuation and grammar. Explain to the children that they are going to write their own setting descriptions as a story opening. Display some of the stimulus images from the CD-ROM (harbour, woodland, playground, shopping centre and busy street) and ask them to choose which setting they want to use.	
Empathy: writing notes based on a first-hand experience will help children understand what characters might be feeling	**Independent work** Ask the children to make notes to use in their writing. Remind them about their earlier work on using the senses. Tell them to make notes of what they can see, hear, smell, touch and how it makes them feel. Ask them to make notes of descriptive adjectives and adverbs to use in their writing.	**Support:** display photocopiable page 23 'Settings' as a reminder for children who need it; some children focus on two senses only
Social skills: listen and respond to other people's ideas; discuss work as a group	**Plenary** Gather the children together and ask for a show of hands for their choices of setting. Group the children together according to same or similar settings choice. Ask them to read and compare the notes they made for the same setting in their groups. Take feedback from each group about the similarities and differences. Ask them to comment on two ideas per group that most impressed them about the notes. Discuss which styles of note-making worked well, for example drawing a spidergram, or grouping ideas in boxes or columns.	

DAY 5 ■ Editing and improving

Key features	Stages	Additional opportunities
	Introduction Ask the children to think about their chosen settings. Tell them to close their eyes for a moment and picture the setting in their heads. With the whole class, ask for quick-fire oral responses. Ask: *What can you see? What can you hear? How does it make you feel?* Explain that the children are going to use their notes from the previous session to start writing their setting descriptions. Ask the children to take ten minutes to write the first draft.	**ICT:** ask the children to use computers to write their descriptions
	Speaking and listening Ask the children to work with a partner and swap their setting descriptions. Tell each pair to read their partner's description aloud, then to discuss each other's writing. Ask them to find two things they can praise, and one aspect for improvement.	
Evaluation: give feedback and judge effectiveness	**Independent work** Ask the children to work at editing and improving their descriptions using the praise and suggestions made during paired work. Ask them to refer to their personal list of success criteria and check their work against it.	**Support:** ask partners to check each other's work against the success criteria
Evaluation: judge effectiveness of own descriptions	**Plenary** Gather the children together and ask volunteers to read their setting descriptions aloud. Encourage the children to suggest what sort of atmosphere the settings have.	

DAY 6 ■ Manipulating images

Key features	Stages	Additional opportunities
	Introduction Explain that the children are going to use their completed setting descriptions to create a visual-and-written description to present the class's work for others to see. Display some of the photographs that were used as stimuli. Ask one of the children who chose a particular setting for their writing to read their setting description aloud. Discuss the mood of their description and compare this with the relevant photograph. Use photo-editing software to manipulate the image to match the mood of the description by altering it from colour to black-and-white or sepia; enlarge aspects of the image or cut parts; lighten or darken the image to show how different effects can alter the mood of the image.	
Evaluation: give feedback and judge effectiveness of own work	Display some of the other images the children used as stimuli and ask them to suggest ways in which the mood can be changed to suit their own descriptions. Encourage some of the children to use the software to alter the mood of the pictures.	
	Independent work Encourage the children to work with a partner and to experiment with altering the images they used as stimuli.	**ICT:** let children who have not done so write up their work on a computer
Communication: communicate outcomes	**Plenary** Ask some of the children to display their setting image and read their description aloud. Discuss what the image adds to the atmosphere of their descriptions.	

DAY 7 ■ Publishing the setting description

Key features	Stages	Additional opportunities
	## Introduction Explain to the children that they are going to complete their setting descriptions and visual images in order to produce a class display. Discuss the effectiveness of including the visual images from the previous session. Suggest that a variety of forms might make the class display more effective. Working with the children, choose two or three of their written pieces of work and experiment with creating a display of written and visual images. Use the manipulated photographs and pictures and also demonstrate how to cut small, mood-creating parts of the whole picture and drop them into the written text using photo-editing and word-processing software to enhance the finished work for display.	
Social skills: work collaboratively in groups	## Independent work Ask the children to work in small groups of two or three and to experiment with creating a screen for a slideshow presentation of their work to include their written descriptions with the digital images. Each of the groups then saves their completed slide to be part of a slideshow of the whole class's work.	**Support:** work with lower ability groups to give them help
Evaluation: give feedback and judge the effectiveness of their own and the class's descriptions	## Plenary Show the completed slideshow to the class and discuss their impressions. Discuss how effective it is, and whether the order should be altered, for example all screens showing one mood followed by another atmosphere, or in a random order. Alter the order of slides to suit their preferences. When complete, arrange for a slideshow for a different class. Print the slideshow to make a permanent wall display.	

Guided writing

Using the notes made for writing a setting description, let the children begin writing their own settings. Ask them to write three different opening sentences. Read the three sentences aloud, asking other members of the group to comment on their preferences. Which are the most effective? Ask the children to use the most effective and continue their setting description. Encourage them to edit their descriptions, checking for errors in spelling and punctuation.

Assessment

Ask the children to look at the photograph of a harbour from the CD-ROM and write a passage to describing a calm setting.
Refer back to the learning outcomes on page 11.

Further work

Provide the children with copies of images of familiar settings. Ask them to annotate the pictures with words and phrases to describe what they see, hear, smell, and touch on the pictures.
In pairs, ask one child to picture a setting in their head and, using the senses, describe it to their partner. The partner then says what they think the setting is.

NARRATIVE ■ UNIT 1

Venn diagram

■ Compare the two settings.

Title: _____

The colour of home

■ 100 LITERACY FRAMEWORK LESSONS YEAR 3

PHOTOCOPIABLE ■ SCHOLASTIC
www.scholastic.co.uk

Name _____ Date _____

Settings

■ Use these ideas to help you describe your setting.
■ Add other words and phrases of your own to the lists.

What can I see?

| colour | buildings | trees | water | people | animals |

_____

What can I hear?

| wind | traffic | talking | music | animals | footsteps |

_____

What can I smell?

| food | smoke | seaweed | grass | fireworks | car exhaust |

_____

How do things feel?

| wet | slimy | crisp | rough | smooth | cold | warm |

_____

How do I feel about it?

| frightened | angry | happy | bored | excited |

_____

Senses

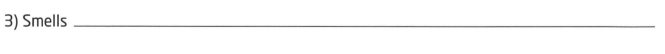

1) Sights _____

_____

_____

2) Sounds _____

_____

_____

3) Smells _____

_____

_____

4) How I feel _____

_____

_____

■ 100 LITERACY FRAMEWORK LESSONS YEAR 3

PHOTOCOPIABLE ■SCHOLASTIC
www.scholastic.co.uk

NARRATIVE
UNIT 2 Myths and legends

Speak and listen for a range of purposes on paper and on screen

Strand 3 Group discussion and interaction
- Use discussion to organise roles and action.
- Actively include and respond to all members of the group.

Read for a range of purposes on paper and on screen

Strand 8 Engaging with and responding to texts
- Identify features that writers use to provoke readers' reactions.

Write for a range of purposes on paper and on screen

Strand 9 Creating and shaping texts
- Use beginning, middle and end to write narratives in which events are sequenced logically and conflicts resolved.

Strand 10 Text structure and organisation
- Signal sequence, place and time to give coherence.

Strand 11 Sentence structure and punctuation
- Show relationships of time, reason and cause through subordination and connectives.

Progression in narrative

In this year children are moving towards:

- Consolidating understanding of sequential story structure: identifying common, formal elements in story openings and endings and typical features of particular types of story; noticing common themes, similar key incidents and typical phrases or expressions.
- Recognising that authors make decisions about how the plot will develop and using different techniques to provoke readers' reactions.
- Making deductions about characters' feelings, behaviour and relationships based on descriptions and their actions in the story; identifying examples of stereotypical characters; making judgements about a character's actions, demonstrating empathy or offering alternative solutions to a problem.
- Learning how settings are used to create atmosphere; looking at examples of scene changes that move the plot on, relieve or build up the tension.
- Telling stories based on own experience and oral versions of familiar stories; including dialogue to set the scene and present characters; varying voice and intonation to create effects and sustain interest; sequencing events clearly and having a definite ending; exploring relationships and situations through drama.
- Writing complete stories with a full sequence of events in narrative order; including a dilemma or conflict and resolution; writing an opening paragraph and further paragraphs for each stage of the story; using either first or third person consistently; using conventions for written dialogue and including some dialogue that shows the relationship between two characters.

Key aspects of learning covered in this Unit

Reasoning
Children will predict and anticipate events in their own quest myth based on the actions of key characters and settings using the language of cause and effect.

Evaluation
Children will express their own views and preferences against agreed criteria to evaluate the work of others.

Empathy
Writing and listening to stories will help children to understand what others might be thinking or feeling in a particular situation.

Social skills
When working collaboratively, children will listen to and respect other people's ideas. They will undertake a variety of roles in group contexts.

Communication
Children will develop their ability to discuss as they work collaboratively in paired, group and whole-class contexts. They will communicate outcomes orally, in writing and through ICT if appropriate.

Prior learning

Before starting this Unit check that the children can:
■ Identify the key elements of a range of settings when discussing a story read on paper or on screen.
■ Understand that a story builds to a climax for a reader, followed by a resolution to the main problem encountered by the central character.
■ Compose and punctuate a simple and a compound sentence.
If they need further support please refer to a prior Unit or a similar Unit in Year 2.

Resources

Phase 1:
The story of Kuang-li part 1 by Gillian Howell ✎; *The story of Kuang-li part 2* by Gillian Howell ✎; *Beowulf and Grendel* by Gill Friel ✎; *The story of Kuang-li part 1* (differentiated) by Gillian Howell ✎; *The story of Kuang-li part 2* (differentiated) by Gillian Howell ✎; Photocopiable page 41 'What sort of story is it?'; Photocopiable page 42 'Myth maker cards'; Myth setting analysis ✎; Quest myth analysis from the PNS website

Phase 2:
Photocopiable page 42 'Myth maker cards'; Quest myth map ✎; Quest myth analysis from the PNS website

Phase 3:
Photocopiable page 43 'Persephone and the pomegranate seeds'; Photocopiable page 44 'Beowulf and Grendel'; Quest myth analysis from the PNS website; Assessment activity 'Settings and characters' ✎

Cross-curricular opportunities

Geography
ICT

UNIT 2 ■ Teaching sequence

Phase	Children's objectives	Summary of activities	Learning outcomes
1	I can read and respond.	Introduce a range of traditional tales, myths and fables. Identify genres.	Children can identify the main features of a quest myth, including the introduction of the characters, the problem to be overcome, the journey undertaken and the resolution of the problem.
		Read the first part of a quest myth. Role play in groups.	
		Read the second part of the quest myth. Summarise the whole story.	
		Read another myth. Identify different sections and summarise it.	
		Identify heroes and monsters from a range of myths.	
	I can explore characters.	Mix and match heroes, monsters and special objects.	
	I can plan elements for a quest myth.	Choose a monster, hero and object. Draw them and add notes. Hot-seat in role.	
2	I can identify settings.	Identify settings and potential dangers.	Children can question others to find out further detail about a narrative tell a story orally, based on their reading, organised in a clear sequence.
		Annotate a quest map. Orally describe a journey and enact it through role play.	
	I can create a group quest map.	Collaborate to choose three settings and create group maps.	
	I can identify problems.	Discuss purposes for the class quest and problems for each setting. Plan how to overcome problems.	
	I can think of a main character.	Choose a hero for the class quest. Choose a hero for the group writing.	
	I can create a file of images.	Model creating a file of images, using ICT. Create their own files in groups.	
	I can create an interactive map.	Model creating an interactive quest map. Create their own in groups.	
	I can tell the quest story orally.	Model telling an oral version of the quest. Create own versions with a partner.	
3	I can begin to write an opening.	Model creating an ICT presentation and write the opening of the class myth. Begin their own in pairs.	Children can write a complete quest myth organised into a clear sequence of events.
	I can contribute to shared writing.	Improve the class myth opening. Plan the introduction of other characters.	
	I can describe characters.	Model character description. Add description to their own presentations.	
	I can write about the purpose.	Model writing the purpose, the first setting and its peril. Add the purpose to their own quests.	
	I can edit and improve.	Model using connectives. Add settings and perils.	
	I can write an ending.	Share the complete class presentation. Write the ending of their own myths.	
	I can present the myth.	Use the Quest myth analysis resource. Enhance their presentations with digital images.	

Provide copies of the objectives for the children.

DAY 1 ▪ Identify different genres

Key features	Stages	Additional opportunities
Social skills: work collaboratively, listen to and respect other people's ideas	**Introduction** Explain to the children that you are going to be exploring different fables, myths, legends and traditional tales. Ask the children to name any they are already familiar with, for example 'The three little pigs', 'Little Red Riding Hood' and ask them to speculate on the type of story they are, from previous reading. Give the children a brief description of the different elements in myth, legends and fables.	
Communication: communicate outcomes orally	**Speaking and listening** Provide a variety of stories for the class, and give each group two or three stories of different genres. Ask the children, as a group, to examine the stories on their table and decide whether each one is a traditional tale, myth, and so on. Ask them to find a reason for their opinions. Invite the groups to move round as a carousel and examine the books on the next table and repeat the exercise. Continue until each group returns to their own table. Ask one group at a time to describe one of the books on their table, to say which genre they think it belongs to and to give a reason for their opinion. Encourage the other children to agree or disagree with the group's opinion. Ask them to describe the main feature that led to the formation of their opinions, for example a hero main character, strange or magical monsters to overcome, stock familiar characters, an element of magic, wishes being granted. Continue until all the story genres have been discussed.	**Support:** use photocopiable page 41 'What sort of story is it?' to sort well-known stories into different genres
	Plenary Read one or two of the shorter myths or legends to the group.	

DAY 2 ▪ Quest myths

Key features	Stages	Additional opportunities
	Introduction Explain that you are going to be reading a quest myth together. Discuss the features that are typical of quest myths, for example a hero or heroine is involved in an adventure that requires them to overcome a monster. Often the quest involves a journey to retrieve an object of great importance or value. Ask them to suggest any quest stories they are familiar with in books or films, for example Greek myths, *Mulan, Harry Potter, The Hobbit* or *Lord of the Rings*. Display *The story of Kuang-li part 1* from the CD-ROM. Read the story with the children and discuss who the characters are and ask them to describe the setting. Remind the children about the work they did on setting descriptions in Unit 1. Ask them to say who the main character is and encourage them to make predictions about what might happen next.	**MFW:** years, animals, whole, white, outside, only, right, without, suddenly, eyes, around
Empathy: understand what others are feeling in a particular situation		**Support:** remind children of key story ingredients; use the differentiated text
Social skills: undertake a variety of roles in group contexts	**Speaking and listening** Ask the children to work in groups and plan a role play enactment of the story so far. Tell them to allot roles: Kuang-li, the headman of the village, the dragon and other villagers. Ask the groups to enact their role plays.	**Extend:** encourage children to use language and vocabulary appropriate to the genre from their experiencing of reading other myths
	Plenary Gather the children together and ask them to describe what happened in their role plays. Encourage them to say which elements of a quest myth are missing from the story so far. Ask some of the groups to perform their role play for the others.	

DAY 3 ■ Key quest elements

Key features	Stages	Additional opportunities
Reasoning: predict events in a quest myth based on the actions of key characters using the language of cause and effect	**Introduction** Remind the children about the story of Kuang-li. Ask the children to predict what they think will happen next in the story. Discuss which of the quest myth elements are missing from the story so far. *How will Kuang-li get to the volcano? What does she need to help her kill the dragon? What will happen to her in the end?* Display the second part of the story from the CD-ROM and read it together. Return to the beginning of the story. Use the questions from the Quest myth analysis resource from the PNS website (there is a web link on the CD-ROM) to discuss and identify the different sections of the story on both extracts. Model how to make notes of some of their findings under the different headings. Keep a copy for reference.	**Support:** identify any difficult or unusual vocabulary before reading; use the differentiated text
Social skills: listen to and respect other people's ideas	**Independent work** Ask the children to write a summary of the story in as few words as possible. Give them a sentence stem such as *The story is about...* Tell them to swap summaries with their partner and compare them.	**Support:** provide a few sentence stems **Extend:** write without having sentence stems provided
Communication: discuss collaboratively in a group context	**Plenary** Gather the children together and ask them to explain how their summaries differ from the story. Encourage them to say what they have left out and what they needed to include in order to still make sense. Ask them how the language has changed in their partner's summary compared to the text. Focus on any summaries that have used phrases such as: *It is set in... The main character is...* Explain that a summary tells them 'about' a story.	**Extend:** invent a new episode for the story describing how the news of the dragon's death reached the village

DAY 4 ■ Analysing a quest

Key features	Stages	Additional opportunities
	Introduction Display *Beowulf* and *Grendel* from the CD-ROM. Tell the children that this is a short version of the story of Beowulf. Read the text together and discuss how this text is different from and similar to the previous quest myth they were reading. Together, identify who the hero is, what the problem to be overcome is, and what object helps the hero. Using the questions on the Quest myth analysis resource from the PNS website, identify any of the different sections in the text. Model noting their findings under the different headings and keep a copy.	**MFW:** great, through, following, mother, only, heard, never **Word-level:** Use the text to explore and collect adjectives for use in future writing
Social skills: listen to and respect other people's ideas	**Independent work** Provide each group of children with copies of the Beowulf text. Ask them to read the text, and then ask each group member to focus on one of the following areas of the story: setting, hero, problem to overcome, magical element or object, outcome. Tell them to note details about it and ask each group member to relate their findings to the group.	**Support:** identify any difficult vocabulary with groups who need extra support
Communication: discuss collaboratively in a paired and whole-class context	**Plenary** Gather the children together and ask one member from each group to share their findings with the class. Discuss any differences that arise. Ask the children to talk with a response partner and each summarise the text from memory.	

DAY 5 ■ Monsters and heroes

Key features	Stages	Additional opportunities
	### Introduction
Explain that the children are going to explore a range of myths to find characters, monsters and objects that they could use as a base for their own quest myths. Ask them to say which ones are their favourite characters, monsters and settings from the myths read so far. Provide a selection of quest myths for the class, including those read in the previous sessions.	**Further information:** explore other myths on the internet or on film and DVD to extend the range covered (copyright permitting)
	### Independent work
Let the children work in small groups and share the stories between them. Ask them to scan the text and illustrations for a monster and a hero that appeals to them. Tell them to make brief notes of what they are and the characteristics or special powers that make them appealing. Ask them to swap stories around and repeat with a different story, until they each have notes about two or three different monsters and heroes. Save the children's notes.	**Extend:** add or choose characters and so on from myths and similar stories from their personal reading and films
Social skills: listen to and respect other people's ideas	### Speaking and listening
Ask the children to tell a partner about their findings and the reasons for their choices.	
	### Plenary
Gather the children together and ask volunteers to describe their favourite choice of monster and hero. Tell them that they do not need to be taken from one story but can be a mixture from different myths. Compare some of the different choices children have made.	

DAY 6 ■ Monsters, heroes and objects

Key features	Stages	Additional opportunities
	### Introduction
Display the notes saved from the previous sessions. Discuss the findings of the class so far under the different headings. Ask the children if they wish to add any further details based on the work they did in the previous session. Explain that they are working towards writing their own quest myths, using the elements they have been exploring. Tell them that today you want them to focus on three key elements: characters, monsters and objects.	
Social skills: listen to and respect other people's ideas	### Independent work
Provide the children with copies of photocopiable page 42 'Myth maker cards'. Ask them to cut out the characters, monsters and objects, mix them up and experiment with grouping them differently. Ask them to choose three and describe each of them to their partner, saying what characteristics they possess and what they look like. Encourage them to speculate about the hero's strengths and weaknesses, why the hero needs to go on the quest, and how they will use the 'object' to help them succeed. Ask them to tell their partner about any other ideas they have for creating a quest featuring their three cards.	**Extend:** encourage some of the groups to use imaginative vocabulary to describe their cards
Communication: communicate outcomes orally	### Plenary
Gather the children together and discuss their ideas. Encourage some of the children to describe their three quest-cards and their ideas for using them in a new myth.	

DAY 7 ▪ Images of monsters, heroes and objects

Key features	Stages	Additional opportunities
	Introduction Explain that today the children are going to choose a final hero, monster and object to use in their own quest myth writing. Tell them they can choose from the myth cards from yesterday's session, the stories they have been exploring in the previous lessons, or they can invent new ones from their own imaginations. Ask them to refer to the notes made before to provide them with ideas and support for their characters.	
Engaging with and responding to texts: identify features that writers use to provoke reactions	**Independent work** Ask the children to draw their hero, the monster and the important object, making notes of characteristics, appearance and special properties, powers and behaviours beside each drawing. Explain that these will be important as part of their plans later.	**Support:** discuss heroes, monsters and objects and scribe their characteristics from the responses
Group discussion and interaction: use talk to organise roles and actions	**Speaking and listening** Ask them to work with a partner and take turns to sit in the hot-seat as their chosen hero or monster. Each partner asks the hero or monster questions about their life, where they live, their habits, what makes them a hero or a monster.	
	Plenary Ask volunteers to role play being their chosen hero or monster for the class, and describe their characteristics to them.	

Guided reading
Choose different myths, legends and traditional tales at an appropriate level for each group. Support the children in identifying text structures and typical language. Ask them to identify main characters, helpers, villains and how the hero overcomes problems. Compare several stories of the same genre. Ask the children to identify any common elements, themes and characteristics of the characters in each story.

Assessment
Discuss the children's learning objectives for the Phase. Ask the children to suggest which objectives they have met and which need further work or improvement.
Have the children been able to identify the differences and common features in different kinds of myths and legends?
Ask the children to summarise the key elements of a quest myth.
Refer back to the learning outcomes on page 27.

Further work
Provide children who are unsure of the features of myths with further examples of myths and legends to read and identify the key elements.
Ask children who need extra practise to summarise the story of Kuang-li.

DAY 1 ■ Dangerous places

Key features	Stages	Additional opportunities
	Introduction Ask the children to think about the settings in *Beowulf and Grendel*. What details about the settings can they recall? Ask them to suggest what was dangerous about the settings to the hero. Note down their suggestions. Use the Myth setting analysis from the CD-ROM to record the Beowulf settings under the headings *Land, Water, Sky* or *Underground*. Remind the children about the story of Kuang-li and repeat the activity. Ask them to suggest which part of the setting posed the most danger for the heroine.	**Support:** provide children with copies of *Beowulf and Grendel* and *The story of Kuang-li*
Social skills: listen to and respect other people's ideas	**Speaking and listening** Ask the children to work in small groups and discuss other quests they are familiar with, from reading or watching film or television. Ask them to identify the key elements of danger in the settings.	
	Independent work Encourage the children to choose a setting from the whole-class and group discussions and write a sentence describing why it posed a danger to the hero or heroine of the story.	
Communication: communicate outcomes orally and in writing	**Plenary** Ask some of the children to read their sentences. Ask the class to suggest which settings appear to be the most dangerous and why. Ask them how the hero or heroine could find a place of safety in some of their choices.	

DAY 2 ■ Quest map

Key features	Stages	Additional opportunities
Reasoning: predict and anticipate events based on settings	**Introduction** Display the Quest myth map from the CD-ROM. Ask the children to describe the island. Encourage them to identify which aspects of this setting could pose a danger to a character in a story. Annotate the map to identify the key places and how they might cause a challenge to the hero. What might potentially occur in these places? Make notes on the map to add details. Ask: *How does the hero reach the island and what potential dangers might occur in this aspect of a setting?* Ask the children to identify areas of the setting which the hero could use as a place of safety and add notes to the map from their suggestions.	
Communication: discuss and collaborate in pairs	**Speaking and listening** Provide pairs of children with a copy of the map. Ask them to discuss how they would travel from the South of the island to the North. Points to consider are: what hazards would be met; how could they avoid, get round or through these hazards; how long would it take them; what might help them along the way. Ask them to work out a role-play journey using the map.	**Support:** ask the children to annotate their copies of the map to use in the role play
Social skills: listen to and respect other people's ideas	**Plenary** Ask some of the pairs to demonstrate their role-play journey to the rest of the class. Discuss and compare their findings about the journey. Discuss whether all or some of these dangerous places should be included in the quest myth story and why.	

DAY 3 ◼ Mapping the journey

Key features	Stages	Additional opportunities
Reasoning: predict events based on settings	**Introduction** Discuss the journey that was planned using the map in the previous session. Ask the children to say which three dangerous places in the map-setting they would like to include in their own writing, and support their opinions with reasons. Ask them to suggest other alternative dangerous settings to use for a quest myth. Write a list of their ideas on the board. Collaborate with the children in choosing three of their ideas that could be part of a quest myth journey for a class story. Model how to draw a map of a journey that includes these three settings. Discuss the length of time it would take the hero or heroine to travel between them and how they would travel, for example using a boat, on horseback, swimming or flying. Annotate the map to show the options.	
Social skills: undertake a variety of roles in group contexts	**Independent work** Ask the children to work in groups and create their own quest map on paper to show the class at the end of the session. Each group member should take on a different role: scribing suggestions, suggesting sounds and sights for each setting of the journey or suggesting specific dangers. One child could observe other groups and borrow their ideas to use in their own group's map.	**Support:** let children use small-world play equipment
	Plenary Ask one member of each group to show their quest map to the other groups and to describe the journey: how the hero travels and the hazards they face in each of the three settings on the map.	**Support:** re-use the Quest myth map from the CD-ROM

DAY 4 ◼ Quest perils

Key features	Stages	Additional opportunities
Reasoning: predict and anticipate events in their own quest myth based on settings	**Introduction** Briefly revise the key elements of a quest myth with the children. Explain that they have been working to create a hero, a monster, settings and a journey. **Speaking and listening** Ask the children to talk to a partner for a few minutes and discuss possible purposes for the quest. Give the children two or three ideas as a stimulus (for example restore a lost treasure, destroy a monster). Take suggestions and list them on the board. Use the Quest myth analysis resource from the PNS website and make notes of their ideas. Add the details of the terrain the hero or heroine had to face in each of the three chosen settings from yesterday's session. Explain that now you have decided on a purpose or problem to solve for the whole quest, you want the children to think about problems they might encounter in each setting. Have a discussion about monsters and perils for each setting and add them to the Quest myth analysis resource. Keep a copy.	
Evaluation: express their own views and preferences against agreed criteria	**Independent work** Ask groups of children to discuss problems for their hero or heroine to encounter in each setting on their own map and how they would overcome them. **Plenary** Ask the children to describe one of their settings and problems to the class. Ask the others to make suggestions of how to overcome the problem for the group's hero or heroine.	**Extend:** ask the children make notes to add to their quest maps

DAY 5 ◼ A special hero or heroine

Key features	Stages	Additional opportunities
Engaging with and responding to texts: identify features to provoke readers' reactions	**Introduction** Ask the children to recall heroes or heroines from the myths they have been reading, and draw up a list on the board. Discuss what special powers, gifts or helpers these heroes and heroines possessed and how they helped them succeed in their quests. Add these to the hero or heroine's name on the list. Discuss how these heroes or heroines would overcome the challenges of the three settings chosen for the class story, by using their strength, weapons, cunning and so on. Return to the class quest myth map and ask the children to suggest which of these heroes they think would be most successful in the setting.	**Support:** provide copies of myths for the children to refer to for ideas and re-use photocopiable page 42 'Myth maker cards'
Text structure and organisation: signal sequence, place and time	**Speaking and listening** Ask the groups to use their quest map drawn up in Day 3. Tell them to choose three different heroes or heroines from known myths drawn up in the whole-class session and discuss how these would overcome the perils and dangers in the three settings on their own quest maps. Ask them to discuss which special attributes they would use and decide together which single hero or heroine would cope best with all three dangerous settings and their monsters or perils. **Plenary** Ask one child from each group to describe the journey the hero makes on their quest map and how the hero overcomes the dangers in each setting. Ask them to comment on each other's ideas and suggest possible improvements.	**Extend:** use temporal connectives to structure their retellings of the journey

DAY 6 ◼ Character file

Key features	Stages	Additional opportunities
Group discussion and interaction: actively include and respond to all members of the group	**Introduction** Explain that the children are going to create an interactive quest map using presentation software which will accompany their final written quest myths and help to structure their ideas. Tell the children they will need to create a file of ideas containing images of characters, settings, monsters and perils and special objects that the main character will meet. Model how to create a file for the class quest myth, using the children's scanned drawings and clip-art. Discuss how to select characters and objects that are appropriate to the settings discussed in previous sessions, for example Beowulf was set in a castle and an undersea cave. Would a dragon or Minotaur work with this setting, or is it more suitable for warriors and magical swords? Model how to make personal choices about what should be contained in the file to suit the setting.	**ICT:** model how to find suitable images online (copyright permitting)
Evaluation: express own views and opinions	**Independent work** Ask the children to work in pairs to research and create a file of images of characters and objects that will challenge and support their hero or heroine during their quests. These could include the drawings created by the children in Phase 1 and clip art. **Plenary** Ask the children to work with a response partner and explain to them how the characters and objects in their file will be used in the setting of their quests. Ask volunteers to give feedback about their file to the whole class. Discuss and compare their different ideas.	**Support:** work with pairs of children who need extra help

DAY 7 ■ Creating an interactive map

Key features	Stages	Additional opportunities
	Introduction Before this session insert a photograph or scanned image of the class quest map into a presentation program file. Demonstrate how to create hotspots that hyperlink to images of characters and objects that will be found in particular areas of the map, using the file of images created in the previous session. Encourage some of the children to help and join in with the demonstration. Discuss how these images could be integrated into the plot of the quest myth, focusing on how they may cause challenges to the hero or heroine, or bring help and support. Remind the children of the notes made on the Quest myth analysis resource to help them make decisions.	
Reasoning: predict and anticipate events	**Independent work** Ask the children to collaborate in groups to create their own interactive map. Tell them to make choices for their hotspots by thinking about how the characters and images will work with the settings to provide challenges and solutions to problems for their hero or heroine during the quest.	**Support:** provide support for those who need it
Communication: communicate outcomes through ICT	**Plenary** Display one of their interactive maps. Allow the children time to explore where the hidden hotspots are and what they contain. Discuss the characteristics of the images and how each of these could be combined to create a quest myth. Ask the children to suggest reasons for the main character being there. What is the purpose of the quest? What will help the hero succeed in his quest? Repeat with one or more of the remaining quest maps	

DAY 8 ■ An oral version of a quest myth

Key features	Stages	Additional opportunities
Engaging with and responding to texts: identify features that writers use to provoke readers' reactions	**Introduction** Display the class interactive quest map. Decide who the central character is and the reason for their being there. Model how to begin an oral telling of the quest, using language to create atmosphere, add description and heighten tension. Encourage children to make suggestions and add details, using the map and images as a prompt.	
Text structure and organisation: signal sequence, place and time to give coherence	**Independent work** Ask the children to work with a partner and collaborate to create an oral version of their own quest myth using their interactive maps. As they work, listen to some of the pairs and encourage them to think about the language and style of their oral versions. Ask questions to stimulate their choices, for example: *How does the hero feel at this point? What do you want the listener to think or feel? How can you make the listener want to find out what happens? What will the final 'big moment' be?* When the children have had sufficient time, ask them to each tell their quest myth to each other.	**Support:** write a selection of connective words and phrases to help children link the sections of their narrative
	Plenary Ask the children to swap partners again and give their new partner time to explore the quest map, find and explore the hotspots, ask questions about the characters and the problems and how they overcome these. Encourage the new response partners to offer feedback and make suggestions for resolving problems and improving the plot. Ask the owner of the map to tell their quest to the new partner.	

Guided reading

Select a myth at an appropriate level for the group. Identify language and sentence structures typical of the genre. Collect time-based connectives used to sequence events. Make a list of connecting words and phrases to use in sequencing an oral version for future use.

Assessment

Observation: Are the children able to work with others? Do they ask questions and make meaningful comments?
Are they able to retell the story orally using a beginning, middle and end?
Are they able to link events using temporal connectives and the language of cause and effect?
Do the children understand how the settings met along a journey can shape the events that occur?
Refer back to the learning outcomes on page 27.

Further work

Ask the children to retell some of their favourite stories using story language. Encourage them to retell stories as a summary, describing what happened in sequence.
Ask them to retell a myth read during guided reading and describe how the setting affected the events.

DAY 1 ■ Creating a presentation

Key features	Stages	Additional opportunities
	Introduction Display the Quest myth analysis resource from the previous sessions and revise the structure of a quest myth with the children. Explain that, over the next few days, the children are going to write their own myths in pairs to go with their maps created in group work. Open the interactive map presentation and add a further five slides, one for each section of a narrative quest: story opening; introduction of characters; main problem or purpose; the journey, settings and perils; the resolution and ending.	
Reasoning: predict and anticipate events	Display the interactive map and encourage the children to describe the quest. Open the first new slide and model how to write an opening for the story. Take suggestions from the class about the sort of language and style to use for the quest, for example *Long ago when knights fought dragons, there...* Encourage the children to experiment with several different opening sentences and type their suggestion on the screen before deciding on the final one. Ask them to add another sentence to the story.	**Support:** refer to other published myths for ideas
	Independent work Ask the children to work with a partner and using their group's quest map as a stimulus, recall the oral versions of the quest. Ask them to begin to write their own opening for their quest.	
Evaluation: express own views against agreed criteria	**Plenary** Ask the children to swap partners and each read their story opening. Ask the new partners to respond to the openings with suggestions for improvement.	

DAY 2 ■ Write an opening

Key features	Stages	Additional opportunities
	Introduction Display the opening screen of the quest myth presentation. Read it to the children and ask them to suggest how it could be improved, based on their independent work in the previous session. Using shared writing, collaborate to extend and improve the story opening by adding two or three more sentences.	**Support:** provide a list of time-based connectives for the children's reference
Reasoning: predict and anticipate events	**Speaking and listening** Discuss how the opening could be further improved by experimenting with connectives to join clauses. Discuss the connectives that could indicate time and draw up a list as a stimulus for independent writing. Return to the interactive map and discuss the characters that are to feature in the narrative with the class. Explore the hotspots and annotate with further details about characters, such as who is introduced first and notes about appearance.	
	Independent work Ask the pairs of children to use their interactive maps to discuss and work out in which order the characters appear, their appearance and any important features that needed for the story. Tell them to make notes of their ideas.	
Social skills: listen to and respect other people's ideas	**Plenary** Ask some of the pairs of children to read their story openings so far to the class and to describe their ideas for introducing the other characters from their notes. Encourage them to sequence their description with temporal connectives, for example *At first, later, finally.*	

DAY 3 ■ Introduce characters

Key features	Stages	Additional opportunities
	Introduction	
	Explain that today the children are going to work on their story openings and introduce the main characters to readers. Display the quest presentation and read the introduction. Open the next slide and using modelled and shared writing, collaborate to introduce the characters and the purpose of the quest. Take suggestions and experiment with adding details – *Jason was tall and strong, the bravest of all...* Read the description to the children and ask them to suggest connectives to help the description flow. Discuss changing adjectives and adverbs. Encourage the children to suggest unusual or powerful descriptive phrases. Return to the story opening and remind the children to continue using a style of language appropriate to the genre, as they discussed in Day 1. Re-read slide two and model how to alter words and phrases so that the style and tone is appropriate for a myth.	
Social skills: listen to and respect other people's ideas		**Support:** provide children with a list of connectives to choose from
	Speaking and listening	
	Ask the pairs of children to describe their main characters orally and collaborate in choosing how they will describe them in writing.	
	Independent work	
Evaluation: express own views and preferences against agreed criteria	Ask the children in pairs to add their character descriptions to their myth.	
	Plenary	
	Ask pairs to swap partners, read their quests so far and suggest improvements.	

DAY 4 ■ Perils and problems

Key features	Stages	Additional opportunities
	Introduction	
Reasoning: predict and anticipate events	Display the Quest myth analysis resource from the PNS website and revise the structure of the quest myth. Focus particularly on the purpose of the quest, and the problems that occur along the journey. Open slide three of the quest presentation and take suggestions of how to introduce the purpose or reason for the quest. Model writing some of the sentences. Open the interactive quest myth map and revisit the hotspots. Focus on the first setting and its perils. Ask the children to suggest ways to describe the setting and introduce the peril or problem it holds for the hero. Model writing their suggestions on slide four of the presentation.	
	Independent work	
	Ask the children to work with their partner and collaborate to add the purpose or reasons for their quests to their myths. Encourage the children to return to the beginning and read through the whole story so far aloud. Remind them to check the style of language and to make use of their own interactive maps and hotspots to help them make use of their planning.	**Support and extend:** mix ability response partners to read and listen to each other's quests, and give feedback
	Plenary	
Reasoning: predict and anticipate events	Ask one of the pairs of children to present their quest myths so far to the rest of the class. Encourage the class to make predictions about the setting they think the characters will encounter next and what dangers it might hold, based on the presentation they are watching. Ask the pair to show their interactive quest map and the first setting hotspot, and then to explain how their hero will handle the problem they have planned for this setting.	

DAY 5 ■ Three settings

Key features	Stages	Additional opportunities

Introduction

Reasoning: predict and anticipate events

Display the class quest presentation and read through the story so far. Return to the opening and read each slide separately. Ask the children to think about how to link the slides using connective words and phrases, for example *suddenly, next*. Take suggestions and model editing the vocabulary to improve the cohesion between sections. Continue to discuss the next setting and its problems along the quest journey. Refer to the interactive map to remind the children of the class plan, and use shared writing to continue the narrative on slide four.

Independent work

Reasoning: predict and anticipate events

Remind the children about yesterday's plenary session. Ask the children to work with their partners. They should revisit their quest maps and write what happens when their main character sets off on the journey and meets the three settings and their problems. Tell them to discuss how the hero will overcome the problems one by one, and to choose vocabulary to describe each peril. Allow them sufficient time to complete this part of their narratives.

Support: work with pairs of children who need extra input

Extend: children who need more space should add extra slides to the presentation

Plenary

Evaluation: express own views against agreed criteria

Ask the children to work with a new response partner and read their myths. Ask them to describe what the best parts are, and make suggestions for improvement. Ask them to return to their usual partner and revise their journey descriptions.

DAY 6 ■ Resolutions

Key features	Stages	Additional opportunities

Introduction

Reasoning: predict and anticipate events using the language of cause and effect

Display the final screen of the Quest myth analysis resource from the PNS website and discuss how the myths they had read before answered these questions. Read the class quest presentation together. Ask the children to suggest how to answer the questions for their own myth. Encourage them to suggest some features of a good story ending and how to use these to conclude the story. Display slide five and collaborate with the class to write the ending of the myth.

Speaking and listening

Evaluation: express own views and preferences

Ask groups of children to work together and share their myths. Ask them to discuss and compare each other's plans for the ending and state their preferences with reasons.

Extend: research myth and legend endings on http:// myths.e2bn.net or search for myths using the local grid for learning website

Independent work

Ask the children to work with their partners to write the resolution and ending to their quest myths.

Plenary

Evaluation: express own views and preferences

Ask some of the pairs of children to read their endings. Ask the others to say which endings they think sound the most effective even though they have been read out of context. Ask some of the authors of the nominated endings to read the whole myth aloud. Discuss whether the children's prior opinions have altered and why. Encourage the children to make any changes to the endings as a result of the others' opinions.

DAY 7 ◾ Myth presentation

Key features	Stages	Additional opportunities
	Introduction Display and read the class quest presentation. Open the Quest myth analysis resource from the PNS website and work through the questions, referring to the class myth. Discuss whether the questions can be answered by the shared narrative. Revise and improve any areas of the writing in the class myth in the light of the questions. Discuss how the myth could be enhanced and published for others to enjoy. Remind the children about the file of images they had created and used in the interactive map. Demonstrate how to copy and insert some of the images onto the screens of the presentation. Encourage the children to give their opinions of the final effect when reading the narrative.	
Evaluation: express own views and preferences against agreed criteria	**Speaking and listening** Direct each pair to exchange their myths with another pair. Ask each group of four to read the myths and evaluate them against the questions on the analysis resource. Take feedback from the groups as a class.	
	Independent work Ask the children to address any issues highlighted in the group activity.	
	Plenary Play the completed class presentation and some of the paired narratives. You could publish the interactive map and quest myth on the school website or the internet.	**ICT:** submit your presentation to your local grid for learning website

Guided writing

Support the children during guided writing to improve their quest myths.
Discuss when the use of connectives would give better cohesion to their writing and improve the fluency.
Identify connectives that demonstrate time, place and cause-and-effect.

Assessment

Provide children with copies of photocopiable page 43 'Persephone and the pomegranate seeds'. Ask them to order the paragraphs to show a clear sequence of events.
Differentiation: Lower ability groups use photocopiable page 44 'Beowulf and Grendel' to reorder the paragraphs
Display the CD-ROM Assessment activity. Children drag and drop the myth characters to the appropriate settings.
Refer back to the learning outcomes on page 27.

Further work

Ask the children, in pairs, to retell myths from their reading, taking turns to tell alternate episodes to show the sequence of events.
Read a myth to the children then use a story circle and ask children to retell the story, continuing the narrative in sequence one after another.
Ask the children to write a diary of their myth with themselves as the central character.

Name _____   Date _____

What sort of story is it?

■ Draw a line to link the story to the right genre. The first one has been done for you.

Genres	Stories
Fairy tale	The three little pigs
	The North Wind and The Sun
Myth	The Peddler of Swaffham
	Beauty and the Beast
Legend	The Boy who cried Wolf
	The Enormous Turnip
	Robin Hood
Fable	Cinderella
	Jason and the Golden Fleece
	The Three Billy Goats Gruff
Traditional tale	The Lion and the Mouse
	Perseus and the Gorgon
	Beowulf and Grendel
	The Legend of Sleepy Hollow
	Sleeping Beauty

Myth maker cards

Monster

Monster

Monster

Object

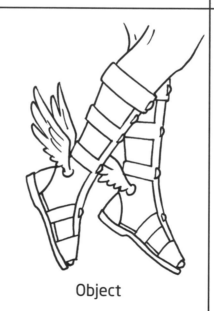

Object

Object

Character

Character

Character

100 LITERACY FRAMEWORK LESSONS YEAR 3

PHOTOCOPIABLE

Illustration © Jon Mitchell / Beehive Illustration.

Persephone and the pomegranate seeds

■ Number the paragraphs 1 to 8 to put them in the correct order.

Demeter was so upset. She searched everywhere but couldn't find Persephone. She was so sad that she forbade the trees and plants to grow while her daughter was missing.

Demeter and Zeus had a beautiful daughter named Persephone. Demeter loved Persephone very much and wanted to keep her near always.

Ever after, there was a winter for three months each year.

So one day, while Persephone was out alone picking flowers, Hades came up from the dark Underworld on his great black chariot and stole her away. But Persephone did not love Hades and to punish him, she decided she would not eat or drink.

Hades, who was God of the Underworld, fell in love with Persephone and wanted to marry her, but Demeter refused to allow it.

Demeter was overjoyed to have Persephone back, but her happiness did not last. Zeus found out that Persephone has sucked on some pomegranate seeds while down in the Underworld. This meant that Persephone had to go back.

Zeus saw how unhappy this made Demeter and Persephone, so he ruled that Persephone should live with Hades in the dark Underworld for three months of the year and nine months above in the sunlight.

Because the plants had all died, people did not have enough food. Therefore Zeus decided that Persephone should come home. There was one condition – she could not have had anything to eat or drink while she was in the Underworld.

Beowulf and Grendel

■ Number the paragraphs 1 to 5 to put them in the correct order.

The next night, Grendel's mother came for revenge! After a great fight, Beowulf followed Grendel's mother to their cave to finish off both monsters.

So Beowulf came to Denmark to help the people overcome the terrible monster. He stayed awake and watched.

One night Beowulf saw the terrible monster. Brave Beowulf fought with Grendel and ripped off one of its legs.

There once was a terrible monster, Grendel, who was killing all the Danes as they slept in the Great Hall of their castle. They needed help.

Suddenly Beowulf saw a huge sword in the cave. He attacked and slew both Grendel and his mother with the sword. Brave Beowulf became a great hero!

NARRATIVE
UNIT 3 Adventure and mystery

Speak and listen for a range of purposes on paper and on screen

Strand 3 Group discussion and interaction
- Use the language of possibility to investigate and reflect on feelings, behaviour or relationships.

Strand 4 Drama
- Use some drama strategies to explore stories or issues.

Read for a range of purposes on paper and on screen

Strand 7 Understanding and interpreting texts
- Infer characters' feelings in fiction and consequences in logical explanations.
- Explore how different texts appeal to readers using varied sentence structures and descriptive language.

Strand 8 Engaging with and responding to texts
- Share and compare reasons for reading preferences, extending range of books read.
- Empathise with characters and debate moral dilemmas portrayed in texts.
- Identify features that writers use to provoke readers' reactions.

Write for a range of purposes on paper and on screen

Strand 9 Creating and shaping texts
- Make decisions about form and purpose; identify success criteria and use them to evaluate their own writing.
- Use beginning, middle and end to write narratives in which events are sequenced logically and conflicts resolved.
- Select and use a range of technical and descriptive vocabulary.

Strand 10 Text structure and organisation
- Signal sequence, place and time to give coherence.
- Group related material into paragraphs.

Strand 11 Sentence structure and punctuation
- Show relationships of time, reason and cause, through subordination and connectives.
- Compose sentences using adjectives, verbs and nouns for precision, clarity and impact.
- Clarify meaning through the use of exclamation marks and speech marks.

Strand 12 Presentation
- Write with consistency in the size and proportion of letters and spacing within and between words, using the correct formation of handwriting joins.

Progression in narrative

In this year children are moving towards:
- Consolidating understanding of sequential story structure; creating suspense.
- Recognising that authors make decisions about how the plot will develop and use different techniques to provoke readers' reactions; noticing the difference between first and third person accounts.
- Making deductions about characters' feelings, behaviour and relationships based on descriptions and their actions in the story.
- Understanding how settings are used to create atmosphere.
- Writing complete stories with a full sequence of events in narrative order.

UNIT 3 ◄ Adventure and mystery continued

Key aspects of learning covered in this Unit

Empathy
By taking part in role-play activities, children will be able to identify with fictional characters and will be helped to understand their feelings and actions.

Creative thinking
Children will use creative thinking to extend and consider alternatives to typical elements of an adventure story and create a new story of their own.

Social skills
When working collaboratively, children will listen to and respect other people's ideas. They will take on different roles in a group.

Communication
Children will develop their ability to work collaboratively in paired, group and whole-class contexts. They will communicate outcomes orally, in writing and through ICT if appropriate.

Prior learning

Before starting this Unit check that the children can:
■ Talk about the similarities and differences in characters, settings and events.
■ Write a complete story with: sequence of events in paragraphs for the opening, problem, resolution, ending; descriptions of new characters or settings; complete sentences in third person and past tense; examples of patterned story language and dialogue with speech marks.
■ Express an opinion and explain a point of view, for example, by using evidence from the text.
If they need further support please refer to a prior Unit or a similar Unit in Year 2.

Resources

Phase 1:
Midnight for Charlie Bone by Jenny Nimmo ❧; *Timid Tim and the Cuggy Thief* by John Prater ❧; *Red eyes at night* by Michael Morpurgo ❧; Photocopiable page 60 'My main character'; A selection of adventure and mystery stories

Phase 2:
Timid Tim and the Cuggy Thief by John Prater ❧; *Red eyes at night* by Michael Morpurgo ❧; Photocopiable page 61 'Writing a letter'; A selection of adventure and mystery stories

Phase 3:
Photocopiable page 23 'Settings'; Photocopiable page 60 'My main character'; Photocopiable page 62 'Adventure stories'; Photocopiable page 63 'Story mountain'; Photocopiable page 64 'Story planning'; A selection of adventure and mystery stories; Assessment activity 'Practice with dialogue – alternative for 'said'' ❧

Cross-curricular opportunities

ICT

UNIT 3 ■ Teaching sequence

Phase	Children's objectives	Summary of activities	Learning outcomes
1	I can read and respond to character.	Shared reading – sit in the hot-seat in role. Write a sentence about a character.	Children can identify key features of adventure stories.
		Explore typical features of characters in adventure stories.	
	I can plan a character.	Model creating a new character. Make notes in pairs.	
	I can understand the effect of setting.	Shared reading – annotate setting description.	
	I can respond to character.	Shared reading – annotate an extract to show character and role play a conversation.	Children can explain reasons why a character has behaved in a particular way.
	I can explore chapter endings.	Whole-class and group discussion about cliffhanger endings.	Children can identify how the author engages the reader and maintains interest.
2	I can use connectives to link paragraphs.	Discuss connectives in adventure stories. Explore how paragraphs are linked.	Children can recount an incident from a story maintaining a first-person viewpoint.
	I can vary the length of sentences.	Explore the use of different sentence types. Write a paragraph.	
	I can describe an event using first person.	Examine point-of-view. Sit in the hot-seat and describe an event from their own point-of-view.	
	I can use present and past tense verbs.	Shared writing to change a third person account to first person. Change verb tenses.	
	I can describe an event using first person.	Model writing a letter in role. Children write a letter.	
3	I can plan characters and settings.	Discuss ideas for settings, heroes and baddies. Draw character and setting in groups.	Children can plan an extended narrative using the key features of the text-type.
		Use character and setting cards to plan a story plot.	
	I can plan a story outline.	Plot the build up of a story on a graph. Plan own stories.	
	I can write a story opening.	Create a list of success criteria. Draft story openings.	
	I can use dialogue.	Shared writing – dialogue. Continue writing stories.	Children can write an extended adventure story with logically sequenced events and a resolution.
	I can improve dialogue.		
	I can make a story exciting.	Class discussion – ways to add excitement. Continue writing stories.	
	I can write a story ending.	Shared writing – a good story ending. Finish their stories.	
	I can polish a story.	Polishing and publishing the stories.	

Provide copies of the objectives for the children.

DAY 1 ■ Adventure and mystery

Key features	Stages	Additional opportunities
	Introduction Explain to the children that you will be exploring adventure stories in the coming weeks. Ask the children to tell you about any adventure and mystery stories they have read or seen. Encourage them to suggest something about the stories that makes them fit into the genre of adventure stories. Read *Timid Tim and the Cuggy Thief* from the CD-ROM to the children. Discuss the main character 'Tim' and ask the children if Tim is a typical adventure story hero. Elicit the fact that Tim is a shy boy and therefore his bravery is unexpected. Ask the children if they have read other adventure stories where the main character behaves in an unexpected way.	**MFW:** night, turned, through, never **Further reading:** provide a selection of adventure and mystery stories
Empathy: take part in role play to identify more closely with fictional characters **Social skills:** work collaboratively in pairs	**Speaking and listening** Ask some of the children to sit in the hot-seat in the role of Tim. Ask the other children to ask 'Tim' about his feelings when his cuggy disappeared, and why he became brave enough to search for it. **Independent work** Ask the children to work with a partner and collaborate together on writing a sentence that describes the character of Tim.	**Early finishers:** choose and read another adventure story
	Plenary Ask some of the pairs of children to read their sentence. Compare and contrast some of their sentences. Begin reading *Midnight for Charlie Bone* by Jenny Nimmo to the class as a serialised story or another mystery adventure story.	

DAY 2 ■ Characters

Key features	Stages	Additional opportunities
	Introduction Remind the children about the main character from yesterday's reading of *Timid Tim and the Cuggy Thief*. Ask a volunteer to describe what has happened so far in *Midnight for Charlie Bone* or an alternative adventure story that you are reading as a serial. Discuss what you know so far about the character of Charlie and ask the children to say if there are any similarities or differences between Charlie and Tim.	
Social skills: listen and respect other people's ideas; take different roles within a group **Communication:** work collaboratively; communicate outcomes orally	**Speaking and listening** Provide a selection of adventure stories for the class. Ask each group to pick two or three different stories. Explain that you want the children to look through the selection of adventure stories and identify the main character. Tell them to scan the text for details about the character. Ask them to discuss what key features they share and any characters that are distinctly different. Can they find anything that all the main characters have in common or that is similar? Ask one member of each group to act as secretary and make notes of their findings.	**Support and extend:** arrange the children in mixed ability pairs to explore different stories
	Plenary Ask a spokesperson from each group to feed back their group's findings to the class. Compare the groups' opinions and ask them to describe any common features they found. Ask them if they think there is a typical hero or heroine in many adventure stories. Discuss any features of a typical hero or main character. Continue reading the class serial.	

DAY 3 ■ Create a character

Key features	Stages	Additional opportunities
Communication: work collaboratively in whole-class contexts	### Introduction Explain to the class that they will be writing their own adventure stories. Discuss the decisions that writers need to make in order to plan their stories, such as who the characters are, where the story is set, how the plot develops. Ask the children to think about a main character for an adventure story. Remind the children about the discussion in yesterday's plenary session about main characters in adventure stories. Display photocopiable page 60 'My main character' to create a character plan using suggestions from the children. Prompt the children with questions and suggestions, for example: *Will the character be shy and become more adventurous, or will he/she be strong and outgoing from the beginning?*	
Empathy: identify with fictional characters	### Speaking and listening Ask the children to work with a partner and discuss the characters from the adventure stories they have been reading in class and independently. Encourage them to say which characters they preferred and why. Ask them to each decide which character attributes they would like to include in their own story writing.	**Support:** children remember characters they have written about before and re-use elements of description that worked well
	### Independent work Provide the children with copies of the photocopiable sheet to make notes about their preferred character.	
	### Plenary Ask the children to describe their favourite character to the class.	

DAY 4 ■ Scary settings

Key features	Stages	Additional opportunities
Empathy: identify with fictional characters and understand their feelings and actions	### Introduction Remind the children of the story *Timid Tim and the Cuggy Thief*. Ask the children to say what the story was about in one sentence. Display *Timid Tim and the Cuggy Thief* from the CD-ROM. Read it together and ask the children to think about the setting at the beginning of the extract. Do they think the setting is safe or scary? Discuss how being tucked up in bed should feel safe and identify how the author makes it scary. Highlight vocabulary that shows this, such as *dark, windy, chilling blast*. Ask the children to say how they would feel in the same setting. Display and read the extract from *Midnight for Charlie Bone* from the CD-ROM.	**MFW:** stopped, suddenly, windows, thought, where, walked
Communication: work collaboratively in pairs	### Independent work Provide a copy of the extract from *Midnight for Charlie Bone* for each child. Ask them to read the extract again and highlight all the words and phrases that describe the setting. Ask the children to go through the extract with a partner, discussing how they feel about this setting, and underlining any examples of how the author uses language to make the reader feel uneasy.	**Support:** children can work in pairs to highlight words about the setting
	### Plenary Invite some of the children to describe how they think Charlie was feeling in the setting of the extract. Ask them how they would feel in the same setting. What is it about the setting that makes them feel this? Continue reading the class serial.	

DAY 5 ■ What happens next?

Key features	Stages	Additional opportunities
Communication: collaborate in whole-class settings	**Introduction** Discuss reasons for events in the adventure stories the children have been reading, for example, ask the children why Tim became involved in his adventure, despite being a shy, quiet boy. *How did Charlie Bone become involved with the mysterious events?* Elicit that something happens in an adventure story which jolts a character to respond. Display the extract from *Red eyes at night* from the CD-ROM. Read it with the children and ask them to suggest how they feel about the two characters in the story. Annotate the extract with notes of their suggestions about the characters' personalities. Point out the first person narrator. Ask how is this story similar and different from the other stories. Ask them to predict what might happen in the rest of the story.	**MFW:** I'm, much, only, never, world, eyes, night **Further reading:** provide copies of *Red eyes at night* by Michael Morpurgo
Empathy: identify with fictional characters through role play	**Speaking and listening** Ask the children to work with a partner and to role play, and continue, the conversation where Millie tells Geraldine about the ghost. Remind the children about their feelings about the two characters from the whole-class discussion and encourage them to take on their character's personality.	**Support:** display the annotated extract created earlier in the lesson
	Plenary Ask some of the children to perform their role play for the others. Discuss their ideas about how the conversation would continue and compare some of their thoughts, particularly focusing on contrasting versions. Continue reading the class serial.	

DAY 6 ■ Chapters and cliffhangers

Key features	Stages	Additional opportunities
	Introduction Remind the children about the extract from *Red eyes at night* from yesterday's session. Focus on how it ended, *Just the ghost.* Ask them to suggest how this ending makes them feel. Elicit that the author wants to make the reader read on to find out what happens next. Explain the term 'cliffhanger' to the children and then read a few chapter endings that have already been read from *Midnight for Charlie Bone* or the alternative class serial. Ask the children to say what effect these endings have.	**MFW:** much, young, night, window, white, right, under **Support:** suggest children look for chapters that end in a question, or a statement about feelings
Communication: work collaboratively in a group	**Independent work** Provide a selection of adventure stories for the groups of children. Ask them to flick through the books and find examples of cliffhanger chapter endings and take turns to read them aloud to their group. Ask the group to choose two cliffhanger endings they think are the most effective.	
Social skills: listen to and respect other people's ideas	**Plenary** Invite each group to read the chapter endings they chose, and ask the rest of the class to say what effect they have. Encourage them to predict what they think might happen next for each chapter ending. Ask the class to suggest which of the chosen endings most make them want to find out what happens next and elicit that the best chapter endings make you keep on reading. Continue reading the class serial.	**Extend:** ask children to find chapter endings that are not cliffhangers but also make the reader want to find out what happens

Guided reading

Select a short adventure story at an appropriate level. Ask children to identify what sort of character the hero is. Encourage them to find evocative language that describes the settings. Ask the children to focus on the chapter endings and those that are cliffhangers. Read the openings of the following chapters and discuss whether the cliffhanger is resolved or if the next chapter still leaves the reader in suspense.

Assessment

Discuss the children's learning objectives for the Phase. Ask the children to suggest which objectives they have met and which need further work or improvement.

Observation: Have the children been able to identify the differences and common features in the main characters of adventure stories? Are the children able to recognise the features of setting descriptions and how they affect characters' feelings and consequent actions?

Refer back to the learning outcomes on page 47.

Further work

Consolidation: Encourage the children to use photocopiable page 60 'My main character' to create additional characters for an adventure story.

Extension: Ask the children to use photocopiable page 60 'My main character' to make notes about characters who are villains in adventure stories.

DAY 1 ▪ Linking paragraphs

Key features	Stages	Additional opportunities
	## Introduction	
	Discuss with the children what they have learned so far about characters, settings and the structure of adventure stories. Talk about how suspense was built in the stories the children have read, for example by revealing more about character and plot as the story develops, and the ending and linking of chapters. Explain how paragraphs within chapters can also build up suspense using connectives.	
Communication: work collaboratively in whole-class and group contexts	Ask the children to suggest some connective words and phrases they have read that they could use in their own writing to build the tension and drive the narrative forward. Together, draw up a list on the board for use in future writing, for example, *suddenly, immediately, all at once, later, instantly, in a flash, slowly, gradually, eventually* and so on.	
	## Independent work	
	Provide groups of children with a selection of short adventure and mystery stories and ask them to look through two or three chapters in the books. Tell them to identify where paragraphs and incidents/events have been linked with connectives that show time. Ask them to put a slip of paper or Post-it Note in the relevant pages in order to share their findings.	**Support:** refer children to the list of temporal connectives used in Unit 2
Social skills: listen to and respect other people's ideas	## Plenary Ask each group to read some of the connective phrases they identified and add any new ones to the list drawn up on the board previously. Talk about how they signal time to the reader. Underline, highlight, or rewrite them according to degrees of difference. Discuss which phrases have the most impact.	

DAY 2 ▪ Altering the pace

Key features	Stages	Additional opportunities
	## Introduction	
	Remind the children about the setting descriptions they wrote in Unit 1. Ask them to recall how they created atmosphere by using the senses in their descriptions. Explain that you are now going to focus on how sentence structures can help to create atmosphere.	
Social skills: listen to and respect other people's ideas	Display the extract from *Timid Tim and the Cuggy Thief* from the CD-ROM. Work through the text, sentence by sentence, and identify with the children which sentences are complex, compound and simple sentences.	**Further reading:** provide a selection of adventure stories
Communication: work collaboratively in whole-class contexts	Focus on the first two sentences of paragraph three. Read the two sentences separately first, then linking them with two or three different connectives, for example: *and, but, however, although*. Ask the children if this has an effect on the atmosphere. Focus on the last two sentences of paragraph three. Rewrite it as one continuous sentence, changing the full stop to a comma. Ask the children how this changes the effect and which they think works better.	and ask children to find longer sentences and shorter sentences. Let them read them to a partner and discuss the effect
	## Independent work	
Creative thinking: extend and consider alternatives to typical elements of adventure stories	Ask the children to imagine their main character is following someone in a dark setting. Ask them to write a paragraph using sentences of different lengths and experiment with how this can change the effect of their writing.	on the pace of the story
	## Plenary Ask some of the children to read their paragraphs aloud. Discuss how longer, complex sentences can slow down the pace, and short sentences can speed it up and increase tension. Continue reading the class serial adventure story.	

DAY 3 ■ First person recount

Key features	Stages	Additional opportunities
Communication: work collaboratively in whole-class contexts	**Introduction** Discuss the stories the children have read so far in this Unit. Ask volunteers to suggest an event or incident in one of the stories that they thought was interesting or exciting and describe it to the class. Ask the children to suggest one main difference between *Red eyes at night* and the other stories they have looked at in detail. Ask them to think about point of view and elicit that it is narrated in the first person, but the others are in the third person. Display the extract from *Timid Tim and the Cuggy Thief* from the CD-ROM. Model how to retell the extract using the first person voice. As you retell the event, ask the children what the main differences are between your oral retelling and the written text.	**Support:** ask the children to retell the extract from *Timid Tim and the Cuggy Thief* using a first person narrator
Empathy: identify with fictional characters through role play	**Speaking and listening** Ask the children to work with a partner and take the roles of two characters from the story of their choice. One character questions the other about an event or incident, and the other answers based on their experiences. Encourage them both to think about how they would feel in the situation they are describing.	**Extension:** let the children do the activity as two characters from different stories
	Plenary Invite some of the children to sit in the hot-seat, and answer questions about their event in role. Encourage the child in the hot-seat to describe how they feel about the event. Ask the class how a first person narrative affects a story. Elicit that readers only see one point of view in detail.	

DAY 4 ■ Different recounts

Key features	Stages	Additional opportunities
Communication: work collaboratively in paired and whole-class contexts	**Introduction** Remind the children about their role play in yesterday's session, such as describing events in the first person. Ask them to think of other ways of recounting an event in the first person and draw up a list of their suggestions on the board, for example diary, biography, letter. Display *Timid Tim and the Cuggy Thief* from the CD-ROM and collaborate with the children in changing it from a third person account to the first person, modelling how to alter proper nouns and pronouns. Ask the children to suggest how it would further change if Tim had written it in a diary, for example informal or incomplete sentences, punctuation and grammar. Display the extract from *Red eyes at night* from the CD-ROM. Focus on the use of the present tense. Ask the children how this affects the narrative (it is informal and conversational in tone).	
	Independent work Provide the children with copies of *Red eyes at night*. Ask them to work in pairs, read each sentence and change the present tense verbs into past tense.	**Support:** ask the children to focus on the first paragraph only
	Plenary Ask the children to say how they think the extract has been affected by altering the verb tenses. Elicit that the words in speech marks still remain in the present tense. Ask them if there were other words that needed to be changed to retain sense in the extract such as *now* as it is time related. Continue reading the class serial.	

DAY 5 ■ Write a letter

Key features	Stages	Additional opportunities
Communication: work collaboratively in whole-class contexts	**Introduction** Discuss the stories read so far and the choices the children made for their role play conversations on Day 3. Ask for suggestions of how their conversational recounts of the events would change if written in a letter to a friend.	
Empathy: identify closely with fictional characters	**Speaking and listening** Using one of the extracts as a basis, model how to write an account of the event in a letter, in the role of a different character, for example the cuggy thief, Geraldine, Uncle Paton. Ask the children to say whether the letter should be written in the first or third person. Encourage the children to make suggestions about sentence structure, punctuation and vocabulary choices as you write. Discuss the tone of the letter. *Is it informal, interesting and conversational? Does it sound like your chosen character?* Ask them to suggest how to achieve an informal tone. Explain that you want the children to choose another character and write their own letter to tell a friend about an event in one of the stories.	**Support:** demonstrate how to set out, begin and end a letter or provide the children with copies of photocopiable page 61 'Writing a letter' to help them structure their writing
	Independent work Ask the children to choose a character and event from one of the stories, and compose a letter to a friend in the role of the character.	
	Plenary Let some of the children read their letters aloud for the class. Ask the children to say if and how their recount has changed the tone of the event.	

Guided reading
Select a short adventure story at an appropriate level. Explore where different types of sentence have been used and the effect on the pace of the story. Identify time-based connectives used to link paragraphs.

Assessment
Observation: Did children vary the sentence lengths of their independent writing and do they understand how this can affect the pace of their writing?
Did the children put themselves in the place of a character to recount the story from that point of view?
Were children able to set out their letters correctly?
Refer back to the learning outcomes on page 47.

Further work
Encourage the children to explore other stories to find examples of long complex sentences that slow down the pace of the narrative, and short simple sentences that increase the pace and tension.
Ask the children to each write a letter to their response partner recounting the same event from one of the stories from a different character's point of view.

DAY 1 ■ Character sketch

Key features	Stages	Additional opportunities
	Introduction Explain to the class that they are going to be planning and writing their own adventure stories over the next two weeks. They will organise their stories into paragraphs or chapters and publish them for other children in the class to read as books or an on-screen story. Explain that, today, they will be working in groups of three to experiment with characters, settings and plots and work out ideas for their stories.	
Communication: work collaboratively in groups **Social skills:** listen to and respect other people's ideas	**Speaking and listening** Ask the children to work in groups of three and discuss ideas for three different settings, three different heroes and three different baddies. Ask them to draw the settings and the characters on separate sheets of paper, and add details that describe them in note form around their drawings. Any groups who think of more than three heroes, baddies or settings should add them to the group's collection.	**Support:** use photocopiable page 60 'My main character' completed in Phase 1, or a new blank sheet for each character; could also use photocopiable page 23 'Settings' from Unit 1 to help them think of settings
Communication: work collaboratively in whole-class contexts	**Plenary** Ask the children to group their drawings into three separate piles, one for settings, one for heroes and one for baddies. Go through them with the class. Identify where similar choices have been made by different children. Choose one from the settings collection, one from heroes and one from baddies and collaborate with the class in thinking of an adventure that might involve all three pictures. Encourage the children to contribute to the plot by discussing what could happen in the chosen setting.	

DAY 2 ■ Create a plot

Key features	Stages	Additional opportunities
Creative thinking: consider alternatives to typical elements of an adventure story	**Introduction** Remind the children about the plenary activity from yesterday's session. Display photocopiable page 62 'Adventure stories' for the class. Explain that this sheet contains a selection of possible heroes, baddies and settings that might feature in an adventure story. Go through each picture with the children and ask them to suggest possible personalities and characteristics that could belong to each hero and baddy. Ask them to suggest what sort of events might occur in each of the setting pictures. Discuss which characters are best suited for some of the different settings and ask the children for reasons for their opinions.	
Communication: work collaboratively in a group	**Speaking and listening** Explain that the children are going to work in groups of three. Provide each group with one copy of the photocopiable sheet. Ask them to cut out the cards, pick out one from each set, and work out an adventure featuring these three ideas. Tell them to repeat the activity two or three times using different cards each time. Ask the group to pick the set of three that they agree had the most potential for featuring in an adventure story.	**Support:** provide children with a limited choice of cards
Social skills: listen to and respect other people's ideas	**Plenary** Ask each group to show their chosen set of cards to the class and explain their ideas for an adventure. Encourage the class to comment on each other's ideas. Make notes of some of the best ideas, and encourage the class to contribute suggestions for improvements. Keep a copy of the notes as a stimulus to help children in their independent writing.	

DAY 3 ◼ Plotting the story

Key features	Stages	Additional opportunities
Communication: work collaboratively in whole class settings	### Introduction Display the notes from yesterday's session. Explain that today the children are going to work with a response partner and begin planning their own individual adventure stories. Remind the children that the audience will be other children in their class. Ask the children to suggest ways in which an adventure story builds, and use their feedback to draw a graph or outline shape to illustrate its development. Encourage the children to think about the story opening (safe, calm setting) a problem, a series of events increasing in excitement that lead to a climax, a resolution and an ending (again calm and safe).	
Social skills: listen to and respect other people's ideas	### Speaking and listening Ask the children to work with a partner and talk about the ideas they had for stories based on the activity they completed in groups of three using the character and setting cards. Ask them to discuss and compare each other's ideas, making suggestions on how their stories could develop.	**Support:** work in a group; use photocopiable page 64 'Story planning' to make notes to plan stories
Creative thinking: create a new story of their own	### Independent work Provide the children with a copy each of photocopiable page 63 'Story mountain'. Ask them to work independently and make notes to plot their story plans on the sheet.	
	### Plenary Ask some of the children to share their story planner with the class. Discuss and compare plot ideas.	

DAY 4 ◼ Success criteria

Key features	Stages	Additional opportunities
Communication: work collaboratively in a whole-class context	### Introduction Remind the children of the typical elements of story writing, such as an opening, a problem, a build up to a resolution and ending. Ask the children what else is needed for a successful adventure story, based on the work they have done in previous sessions. Take suggestions and write them on the board. Encourage the children to think about paragraphs and connectives to signal time and place, how dialogue can move the plot forward, how to include setting or character description. Discuss the elements on the board and rewrite them as a list of children's targets for success. Explain that today they are going to be writing drafts of their stories and the focus will be on writing the story opening. Ask the children to suggest different ways of beginning their stories and draw up a list of two or three, for example: setting description, dialogue, character description.	**Extend:** children could explore the adventure stories to find different ways of opening their story
Creative thinking: create a new story of their own	### Independent work Ask the children to refer to their story plans on photocopiable page 63 'Story mountain' and begin writing the opening for their adventure story in draft form.	
	### Plenary Read some of the story openings aloud to the class. Discuss and compare the types of story openings the children chose. Encourage them to suggest what they think might happen. Ask the children to suggest two things about the story openings that they think work well. Continue the class serial if time allows.	

DAY 5 ◼ Dialogue

Key features	Stages	Additional opportunities
Communication: work collaboratively in whole class contexts	**Introduction** Explain that you are going to focus on the part dialogue plays in an adventure story as a whole class and later the children are going to continue writing their stories independently. Ask the children to suggest reasons for adding dialogue to their stories. Elicit that it adds interest, tells the reader what characters are thinking and moves the plot forward in an interesting way. Write a short piece of dialogue on the board, such as – *he has stolen the key she said* – without punctuation and using the reporting clause *she said*. Ask the children what punctuation is needed and where it should go and add it into the sentence. Focus on the word *said*. Encourage the children to suggest other more powerful verbs to replace *said* and experiment with changing the atmosphere and meaning. Ask them how using *whispered* changes the effect compared to *yelled*.	
	Independent work Invite the children to continue their stories. Observe and support them as they write. Those children who have finished their story openings could write them on the computer, before continuing.	**Extend:** ask the children to begin writing their story using presentation software
Social skills: listen to and respect other people's ideas	**Plenary** Ask the children if any of them have more than two characters in their stories. Ask them to describe the extra character or characters to the class. Discuss what sort of conversations these characters have. Remind the children that the dialogue should contribute to the story and not be just general chat.	

DAY 6 ◼ Adding interest with dialogue

Key features	Stages	Additional opportunities
Social skills: listen to and respect other people's ideas	**Introduction** Explain that you are going to look at ways to make the dialogue in their stories more interesting to readers. Write several pieces of dialogue on the board in varying styles, for example: *As they ran, he told her about the secret entrance to the castle. 'Do you mean we have to go through that awful tunnel?' she gasped.* Ask the children to suggest what this tells readers about the story, particularly about the second character. Experiment with adding an adverb or phrase to the reporting clause for different effects, for example *puffing* would show that she is out of breath; *as they approached the iron gateway* tells readers where the characters are now. Repeat with other short pieces of dialogue and take suggestions from some of the children's own dialogue.	
Communication: collaborate when working in pairs	**Speaking and listening** Let the children work with their response partner and read the dialogue they wrote in the previous session using expressive tones. Ask them to discuss alternative reporting clauses to improve the dialogue.	**Support:** provide a thesaurus to help children find alternative vocabulary
	Independent work Ask the children to continue writing their stories. Work with individual children to support them in moving the plot forward.	**ICT:** continue stories on computer or as a presentation
	Plenary Ask the children who think they have improved their dialogue to read it aloud to the class.	

DAY 7 ■ Exciting stories

Key features	Stages	Additional opportunities
	### Introduction Remind the children about the adventure stories they read in Phases 1 and 2 of the Unit. Ask them to say which ones they thought were the most exciting. Create a list of features that made these stories exciting. Discuss how the authors achieved the feelings of excitement, tension or suspense, for example by using cliffhanger endings to paragraphs and/or chapters, by using varied sentences to describe settings, characters and action, to speed up or slow down the pace of the narrative. Explain that they can often show their readers how a character feels in a situation by describing how they speak, or act, rather than saying it directly. A line such as 'his hand shook as he reached to grasp the key' shows that the character is nervous or frightened or excited. Ask the children to re-read and check their writing so far to find passages of the narrative they could improve by using any of the devices just discussed.	**ICT:** use ICT to write their stories
Creative thinking: extend and consider alternatives to typical elements in their story writing	### Independent work Let the children continue writing, re-reading and checking their adventure stories. Ask them to check how their paragraphs or chapters are linked and ended. Ask them to look for ways to use cliffhanger endings to add suspense. ### Plenary Go through the list of features and devices discussed in the whole-class session one at a time. Ask any children who made use of them to describe what they did and how they think it improves their stories.	**Support:** give support to individual children who need it in improving their narratives

DAY 8 ■ Story endings

Key features	Stages	Additional opportunities
	### Introduction Explain to the children that you want them to aim to finish their stories today. Ask them to suggest ways of ending stories, based on the adventure stories they have been reading in this Unit. Encourage the children to recall how the stories they have been reading were ended. Discuss which endings they preferred and why. Remind the class about how not to end their stories, such as *they all went home, the end, it was only a dream.* Read some closing paragraphs from the adventure stories to the class. Ask the class if there are any elements of these endings they think would be suitable for their own stories. Invite some of the children to share their ideas about how they will end their own stories with the class.	
Creative thinking: create an ending to an adventure story of their own	### Independent work Ask the children to finish their stories on paper, as presentations and using word processing. ### Plenary Ask the children who have completed the endings to their stories to read through them and check for sense, spelling and punctuation.	**Support:** ask pairs of children to read and comment on sense, spelling and punctuation of each other's work

DAY 9 ■ Presentation

Key features	Stages	Additional opportunities
Communication: collaborate when working in a whole-class context	**Introduction** Explain to the class that they are going to polish their stories and think of how best to present them as completed work to be read by others. Ask the children for suggestions, for example, should the stories be all written on paper as short books, put onto presentation software or written on a computer, or a combination of methods? Invite the children to discuss with a response partner and decide how their work will be presented.	
	Independent work Ask the children to re-read and put any finishing touches to their stories. Divide the class according to the way their story will be presented and ask them to finish their screen based, word-processed or hand written stories as polished pieces of writing.	**Further reading:** keep all the finished adventure stories available for children to read at another time
Social skills: listen to and respect other people's opinions	**Plenary** Review the success criteria for the Unit with the children. Ask the children to work with their response partner and read their stories aloud to each other. Ask the partners to give feedback based on the success criteria.	

Guided reading and writing
Work with groups of children in guided writing, focusing on aspects of their adventure stories that need support and improvement.
Focus on aspects of adventure stories individually, such as identify where an author uses effective dialogue and why; identify where an author builds suspense and how it is achieved; identify where sentence structures are varied and the effect on pace.

Assessment
Peer assessment: Assess final work based on agreed success criteria.
Discuss success criteria with the class and identify areas that need further work.
Use the assessment activity on the CD-ROM to assess use of dialogue.
Refer back to the learning outcomes on page 47.

Further work
Ask the children to work with a partner and retell their adventure stories using a first person viewpoint.
Let the children read their stories to children from another class.
Encourage the children to compare the adventure stories with the class serial, a mystery adventure. Discuss similarities and key differences in style.

My main character

■ Make notes to describe your character.

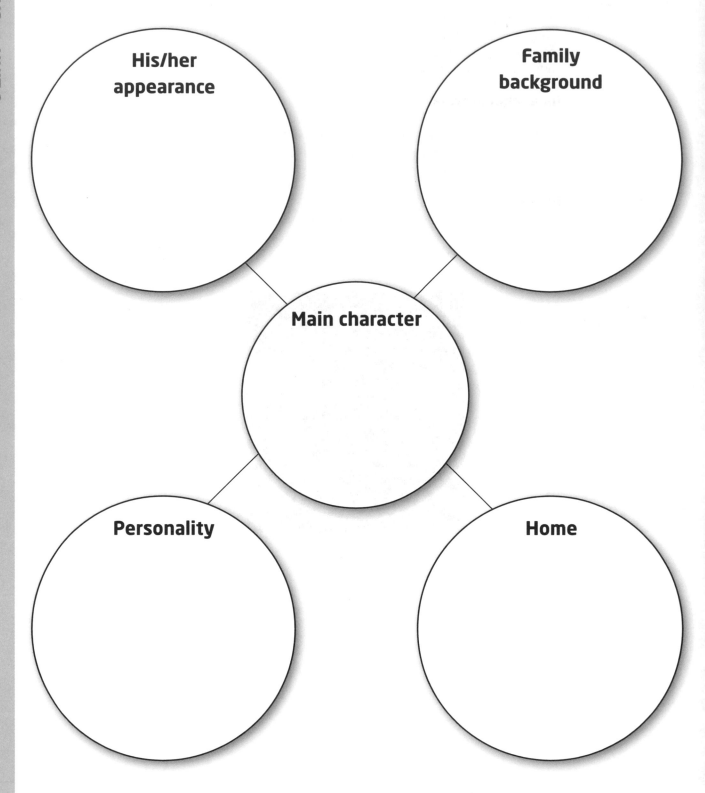

His/her
appearance

Family
background

Main character

Personality

Home

Writing a letter

Your address

_____

_____

_____

_____

Date   _____

Dear _____

How are you? Just wait 'til you hear what happened…

_____

_____

_____

_____

_____

_____

_____

_____

I bet you can't wait to find out how it all ends! Me too!

Love from

_____

Adventure stories

Story mountain

■ Note the events in the story that show how the plot changes in level of tension.

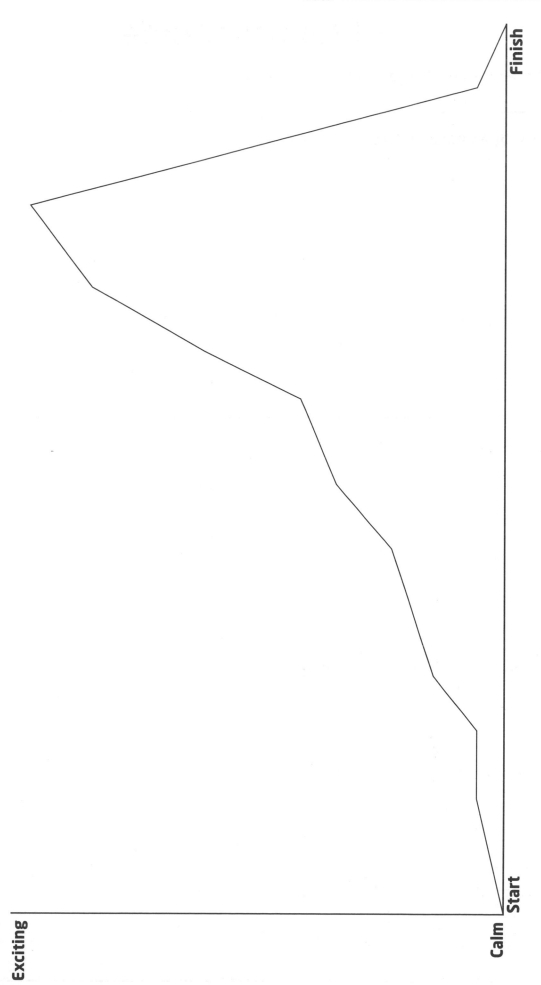

Exciting

Calm

Start

Finish

Story planning

■ Make notes to plan your story using the table.

Story Opening: Introduce your main characters and setting.
Problem: Introduce the problem or dilemma for your main character.
Events: Describe a series of events leading to a climax. 1. 2. 3.
Climax: This is the most exciting part!
Resolution: How your main character solves the problem.
Ending: What happens after the problem has been solved.

NARRATIVE
UNIT 4 Authors and letters

Speak and listen for a range of purposes on paper and on screen

Strand 1 Speaking
- Sustain conversation, explain or give reasons for their views or choices.

Strand 3 Group discussion and interaction
- Use discussion to organise roles and action.
- Actively include and respond to all members of the group.

Read for a range of purposes on paper and on screen

Strand 7 Understanding and interpreting texts
- Explore how different texts appeal to readers using varied sentence structures and descriptive language.

Strand 8 Engaging and responding to texts
- Share and compare reasons for reading preferences, extending range of books read.
- Identify features that writers use to provoke readers' reactions.

Write for a range of purposes on paper and on screen

Strand 9 Creating and shaping texts
- Use layout, format, graphics and illustrations for different purposes.

Strand 10 Text structure and organisation
- Group related material into paragraphs.

Strand 11 Sentence structure and punctuation
- Compose sentences using adjectives, verbs and nouns for precision, clarity and impact.

Strand 12 Presentation
- Write with consistency in the size and proportion of letters and spacing within and between words, using the correct formation of handwriting joins.
- Develop accuracy and speed when using keyboard skills to type, edit and re-draft.

Progression in narrative

In this year children are moving towards:
- Consolidating understanding of sequential story structure: identifying common, formal elements in story openings and endings and typical features of particular types of story; noticing common themes, similar key incidents and typical phrases or expressions.
- Recognising that authors make decisions about how the plot will develop and use different techniques to provoke readers' reactions; noticing the difference between first and third person accounts; taking part in dramatised readings using different voices for the narrator and main characters.
- Making deductions about characters' feelings, behaviour and relationships based on descriptions and their actions in the story; identifying examples of stereotypical characters; making judgements about a character's actions, demonstrating empathy or offering alternative solutions to a problem; analysing the way that the main character(s) usually talks and look for evidence of the relationship between characters based on dialogue.
- Understanding that settings are used to create atmosphere; looking at examples of scene changes that move the plot on, relieve or build up tension.

▶

UNIT 4 ◄ Authors and letters *continued*

■ Telling stories based on own experience and oral versions of familiar stories; including dialogue to set the scene and present characters; varying voice and intonation to create effects and sustain interest; sequencing events clearly and have a definite ending; exploring relationships and situations through drama.

Key aspects of learning covered in this Unit

Reasoning
Children will learn about gathering evidence to support their opinions about books and giving reasons when they state their point of view to the class or group.

Self-awareness
Children will discuss and reflect on their personal responses to texts read.

Social skills
When working collaboratively children will listen to and respect other people's ideas. They will take on different roles in a group.

Communication
As they learn the conventions of letter writing, children will begin to appreciate the need to vary tone and content according to audience and purpose. They will communicate outcomes orally, in writing and through ICT if appropriate.

Prior learning

Before starting this Unit check that the children can:
■ Talk about a particular author and the type of books that author writes; express a personal response and make independent choices about their own reading.
■ Make a valid contribution to a collaborative group activity, listen to others and reach agreement within the group.
■ Write and punctuate simple, compound and some complex sentences.
■ Group sentences into paragraphs.
If they need further support please refer to a prior Unit or a similar Unit in Year 2.

Resources

Phase 1:
Daggie Dogfoot: Taken Away by Dick King-Smith ✺; *A Mouse called Wolf* by Dick King-Smith ✺; Photocopiable page 78 'Story Summary'; Photocopiable page 79 'The work of Dick King-Smith'; Photocopiable page 80 'Book review'; Photocopiable page 81 'Book review writing frame'
Phase 2:
Dear Miss Perfect by Gillian Howell ✺; Photocopiable page 61 'Writing a letter'; Photocopiable page 82 'Traffic safety'; Sample letters from various sources
Phase 3:
Assessment activity 'Dear Mr King-Smith' ✺

Cross-curricular opportunities

ICT
Citizenship

UNIT 4 ■ Teaching sequence

Phase	Children's objectives	Summary of activities	Learning outcomes
1	I can learn about an author.	Shared reading of Dick King-Smith story. Write a sentence to summarise the opening.	Children can explain why they like books by a particular author, referring to an author's style or themes.
		Compare two story openings with a partner.	
		Shared reading – begin a comparison chart of stories by Dick King-Smith.	
		Research Dick King-Smith in groups.	
	I can write a book review.	Model writing a book review. Write a book review.	
	I can learn about another author.	Choose a different author. Work in groups to research a new author.	
	I can write a book review.	Write a book review for the author of their choice.	
	I can present a book review.	Present book reviews and evaluate them.	
2	I can understand how letters are structured.	Shared reading – sequence paragraphs of a letter.	Children can identify the key features of different types of letters.
	I can the understand the difference between formal and informal letters.	Work in groups to identify formal and informal features of letters.	
3	I can write a letter to an author.	Model writing a letter to an author. Choose an author and make notes with a partner.	Children can write a letter for a specific purpose and audience.
		Write a draft letter.	
		Write a polished version.	
	I can write a letter to a friend.	Model writing a letter to recommend a book. Make notes.	
		Compare two letters. Complete and send a letter.	

Provide copies of the objectives for the children.

DAY 1 ■ Favourite authors

Key features	Stages	Additional opportunities
	Introduction Explain to the class that you are going to be exploring the stories of favourite authors. Ask the children to suggest what their favourite book is and who their favourite authors are. Discuss and compare the children's choices. Display the extract *Daggie Dogfoot: Taken Away* from the CD-ROM. Read the text together, without telling the children the title or the author's name. Ask the children how the story opens (uses dialogue). Ask them to look at the next piece of dialogue and say what it contributes to the story (for example confirms the opening and the use of the word *dag*). Make a selection of stories written by Dick King-Smith available for the children.	**MFW:** during, first, brother, sister, different, mother, morning, eyes **Revision:** remind the children about their work on dialogue from the previous Unit
Social skills: listen to and respect other people's ideas	**Speaking and listening** Provide the children with copies of the extract. Ask the children to work with a partner and discuss the story extract. Ask them to find out what they think the setting is; what sort of characters there are and to predict how they think the story will develop. Ask them to think of any features which they think might be typical of this author.	**Extend:** write a paragraph to summarise the extract
Self-awareness: reflect on their personal responses to texts read	**Independent work** Ask the children to write a sentence describing what happens in the story opening. **Plenary** Ask some of the children to read their sentences and summaries to the class.	**Support:** give children a sentence stem and use photocopiable page 78 'Story summary'

DAY 2 ■ Dick King-Smith (1)

Key features	Stages	Additional opportunities
Reasoning: gather evidence to support their opinions and give reasons for their point of view	**Introduction** Display the story opening from *A Mouse called Wolf* by Dick King-Smith from the CD-ROM. Read the extract together. Focus again on the spoken words and discuss how they contribute information to the story. Ask the children how this story opening differs from the story opening read yesterday (it begins by describing a key character, while the previous opening began with dialogue). Ask them to suggest how this story is similar to the previous one. Elicit the response that the characters are both animals, the settings are both the animals' homes and the main character is the last, smallest baby in a litter. Ask the children to predict what they think might happen in this story. Tell the children that both stories were written by Dick King-Smith. Ask the children what other stories they have read by this author.	**MFW:** children, mother, brothers, sisters, lady, before, gone, through, paper
Self-awareness: discuss and reflect on their personal responses	**Speaking and listening** Ask the children to work with a partner and choose one book from the class display. Ask them to read the opening of the story and compare characters and setting with the two openings that were read in the whole-class session. Ask them to look briefly through the story and talk about what happens, and if they think they would enjoy reading the entire book.	**Extend:** choose a different story by the author to read independently
	Plenary Take feedback from the children about their impressions of the stories. Explain that you are going to be exploring other stories by this author and finding out about him and his writing. Begin reading one of his books as a serial.	

DAY 3 ■ Author style

Key features	Stages	Additional opportunities
Reasoning: give reasons to support opinions	### Introduction Begin by reading another chapter of the Dick King-Smith serial story to the class. Discuss the sort of story this is and compare it to the story openings read in the previous two sessions. Ask the children to describe the setting and the characters. Invite them to suggest similarities between the three stories. Ask the children which aspects of the stories they most enjoy. Encourage the children to give their personal opinions rather than just agreeing with the rest of the class.	
Social skills: respect other people's ideas	### Speaking and listening Ask the children to work with a response partner and choose a different book, as yet unread, from the class display. Let them read the title and back cover blurb and predict what they think the story will be about. Ask them to flick through the book to confirm their opinions. Tell them to identify any aspects this book has in common with the others already explored.	**Extend:** copyright permitting, watch the film *Babe* with the class (based on Dick King-Smith's *The Sheep-Pig*)
	### Independent work Ask the children to fill in the chart on photocopiable page 79 'The work of Dick King-Smith' with their findings about the books they have read or dipped into by Dick King-Smith so far.	
	### Plenary Ask the children to describe any common features in the stories they have read so far. They can use their charts to help them explain their ideas. Continue reading the class serial.	

DAY 4 ■ Author research

Key features	Stages	Additional opportunities
	### Introduction Talk with the children about what they already know about the stories written by Dick King-Smith. Ask them to suggest other things they would like to find out, for example, what other stories he has written, how he became a writer, which are his favourite stories, what books he likes to read and so on. Explain to the class that they are going to research more information about Dick King-Smith. On the board, draw up a list of areas for research and questions they would like answers to. Divide the class into three groups. Ask one group to use the internet to research answers to the questions; one group to research biographies and another to research back-cover blurbs in the class collection.	**ICT:** listen to a Dick King-Smith audio book
Social skills: take on different roles in a group	### Speaking and listening Ask the children to collect their research findings as a group and assign one member to act as secretary and make notes.	
Social skills: listen to and respect other people's ideas	### Plenary Gather the children together, and ask a child from each group to report their findings to the other groups, using the secretary's notes. Discuss and compare the information found by the different groups. Ask them to suggest which method was the most productive and enjoyable. Together, discuss what they would like to know that they have not yet discovered and draw up a class list of questions they would like to ask the author. Keep a copy of the questions for use in Phase 3 of the Unit. Continue reading the class serial	

DAY 5 ■ Dick King-Smith (2)

Key features	Stages	Additional opportunities
	Introduction Discuss *A Mouse called Wolf* with the children. Ask for their opinions about it and display the review on photocopiable page 80 'Book review'. Explore the contents: a summary, highlighting features and recommendations. Discuss which stories by Dick King-Smith were the children's favourites. Choose one from the suggestions and model how to write a book review to recommend it to other children. Model how to organise the layout of the review, how to summarise the content and to highlight features that you particularly enjoyed. Ask for suggestions from the class about sentence structure, spelling and punctuation as you write.	
Social skills: listen to and respect other people's ideas	**Speaking and listening** Ask the children to work with a response partner and choose one story they both enjoyed. Ask them discuss the story and favourite features and to make notes about the story to plan a book review based on the whole-class session.	**Support:** use photocopiable page 81 'Book review writing frame' to structure notes and/or written reviews
	Independent work Encourage the children to work independently to write a book review using the notes they made during paired work.	
Social skills: listen to and respect other people's ideas	**Plenary** Ask some pairs of children to read their book reviews and discuss how similar or different both versions are. Collect their book reviews as a class display or as a collection of book reviews for reference. Continue the class serial.	

DAY 6 ■ Research a new author

Key features	Stages	Additional opportunities
	Introduction Explain to the class that they are going to research information about different authors. Remind the class about the favourite authors they discussed in the first session of this Unit; ask them to suggest any other authors they would like to research and draw up a list on the board.	
Social skills: listen to and respect other people's ideas; take on different roles in a group	**Independent work** Divide the class into groups. Ask the children to choose one author for their group, trying to ensure that each group works on a different author. Provide a selection of works written by each author for the groups. Ask the groups to select a chairperson. This person will allocate different roles and methods of researching the information, for example books, back covers, biographies and the internet, to include each member of the group. The chairperson will also select one person to act as secretary to collate their findings. Try to provide several copies of one title per group so they can read and discuss the same story. Ask the group secretary to write notes for the group.	**Support and extend:** ensure groups are of mixed ability
Reasoning: gather evidence to support their opinions about books and give reasons	**Plenary** Gather the children together and ask each group's chairperson to describe how their group approached the task, which author they researched and give an oral summary of their findings. Discuss and compare how easy or difficult it was to collect information about their chosen authors. Continue the class serial.	

DAY 7 ■ Other authors

Key features	Stages	Additional opportunities
Self-awareness: discuss and reflect on personal responses to texts read	**Introduction** Explain that the children are going to write a book review of their group's favourite book, based on the research and collaboration they did in the previous session. Ask the children to suggest what content they should include and the order and layout of their reviews. Remind them of the reviews they wrote for the Dick King-Smith book and ask them if there is any extra information they feel should be included. If necessary, display photocopiable page 80 'Book review' and talk through the layout, organisation and content with the class.	
Reasoning: gather evidence to support their opinions about books and give reasons	**Speaking and listening** Ask each group to review their reading and research from yesterday and together decide on the group's favourite title. Ask them to discuss the information they should include in a review of their favourite book and each make notes.	**Support:** use photocopiable page 81 'Book review writing frame' to structure their writing
	Independent work Ask the children to each write a review of the book that their group chose, using the notes they made together. Ask them to polish their writing, either on paper or on screen.	**Extend:** ask the children to enhance their finished work with images
	Plenary Ask the children to return to their groups and swap reviews. Tell them to read and compare each other's work and make final edits as needed.	

DAY 8 ■ Recommending a book

Key features	Stages	Additional opportunities
	Introduction Explain that in today's session each group is going to be presenting their book reviews to the whole class.	
Social skills: listen to and respect other people's opinions	**Speaking and listening** Ask each group to appoint a spokesperson. Ask the spokesperson to describe the book chosen by their group and the reasons why they chose it. They should explain to the class why they think others in the class will enjoy reading it. Allow time for the spokesperson from each group to describe their chosen title.	**Further reading:** collect and display book reviews from newspapers and magazines
Reasoning: give reasons when they state their point of view	**Independent work** Collect all the written reviews. Ask the children to read at least two reviews from each group, and to watch those reviews presented on screen. Ask the children to work with a response partner and describe the book reviews that they found most interesting. Tell them to compare each other's choices and give reasons for their personal choice of book they want to read. Encourage the children to consider which book reviews they find the most interesting and why.	**Display:** collect the book reviews to display as a book of reviews with those written about Dick King-Smith
	Plenary Gather the class together and ask the children whether reading the book reviews has helped them to choose books they might not otherwise have thought of reading. Ask them which titles they chose, and why the review helped them to make the decision.	

Guided reading

Select a Dick King-Smith story at an appropriate level for the group. Focus on the author's use of dialogue to give information about the plot to the reader. Ask the children to identify punctuation used to denote dialogue.

Work with children during guided writing to help them use a variety of descriptive words and phrases in their book reviews.

Assessment

Observation: Are the children able to give evidence to support their opinions about authors and books? When working in a group situation, do individual children make a contribution?

Refer back to the learning outcomes on page 67.

Further work

Ask the children to use photocopiable page 79 'The work of Dick King-Smith' to make notes and compare other books by different authors that they are reading independently.

Encourage the children to use photocopiable page 81 'Book review writing frame' to write book reviews on titles they read independently.

DAY 1 ■ Letters

Key features	Stages	Additional opportunities
	Introduction Before beginning this Phase of the Unit, ask the children to bring a letter from home (with permission) that they or their parents/carers have received. Explain that you are going to be examining letter writing for different purposes so they can bring in any kind of letter they choose. Collect other examples of letters from newspapers and so on. Discuss what the children know about the purpose of letters. Draw up a list on the board from their suggestions (letters to complain, thank, congratulate, invite, recount, accept an invitation). **Self-awareness:** reflect on personal responses to texts read	
Self-awareness: reflect on personal responses to texts read	Display the letter *Dear Miss Perfect* from the CD-ROM. Read it together and ask the children to say what the purpose of the letter is (to thank and to invite). Explain the layout of the letter, the greeting and how it is signed. Discuss each paragraph and ask the children to suggest what the purpose is. Ask them to suggest what might be in the reply.	
Social skills: listen to and respect other people's ideas	**Independent work** Cut copies of the letter on photocopiable page 82 'Traffic safety' into sections and give to pairs of children. Ask them to read and organise the sections of the letter so that it makes sense.	**Support:** use photocopiable page 61 'Writing a letter' from Unit 3
	Plenary Ask some of the children to read their reorganised letters. Discuss the purpose of the sections, and of the whole letter. Ask the children about similarities and differences between this letter and the one read before, for example: purpose, more formal tone, different way of greeting and of signing off.	

DAY 2 ■ Formal and informal letters

Key features	Stages	Additional opportunities
	Introduction Arrange the children in groups and provide them with a selection of the letters they have brought, and letters from newspapers and magazines.	**Support and extend:** arrange the children in mixed-ability groups
	Speaking and listening Invite the groups to read and discuss the purpose of the letters and to group them according to type.	
Social skills: listen to and respect other people's ideas	**Independent work** Let the groups choose two different letters, one formal and one informal. Ask them to read the letters carefully and identify how the formal or informal tone is achieved, such as how the sentence structures differ, how punctuation has been used, how the vocabulary differs. Ask them to highlight or underline a formal and an informal sentence, formal and informal greetings and signings off and informal uses of punctuation. Ask them to note what is similar or consistent about the layouts of the letters.	
Communication: begin to appreciate the need to vary tone and content according to audience and purpose	**Plenary** Taking formal writing first, ask the children to describe the formal letter they studied, its purpose and the features of its sentence structures. Repeat with informal letters. Ask the children to suggest the key differences in these styles of letter writing, Elicit that an informal tone is used when you know the recipient, and a formal tone for an unknown recipient.	

Guided reading

Use some of the letters that are at an appropriate level in guided reading. Focus on verb tenses, connectives and use of paragraphs.

Assessment

Observation: Are the children confident in the layout and structure of letter writing?

Do children recognise how purpose and audience affects the tone of the letter?

Refer back to the learning outcomes on page 67.

Further work

Ask the children to revise the layout and structure of letters using photocopiable page 61 'Writing a letter' from Unit 3.

DAY 1 ■ Letters to real people

Key features	Stages	Additional opportunities
	### Introduction Tell the class that they are going to write their own letters to an author. Explain that you are going to demonstrate how to write to an author using Dick King-Smith as an example. Remind the children about the questions they thought of in the plenary session of Day 4 in Phase 1 of this Unit. Display the list and ask if there is any other information they would like to know. Add any of the children's suggestions to the list. Demonstrate how to make notes about what you want to say in the letter, for example what you enjoy about the author's books, particular titles you have read and questions you would like to ask. Begin to model writing the letter and rehearse sentences orally, for example: *Should I start with Dear Dick, or Dear Mr King-Smith?* Discuss the order in which you want to use your notes and how to group them into paragraphs. Keep a copy for future reference.	
Self-awareness: discuss and reflect on personal responses to texts read	### Speaking and listening Invite the children to work with a response partner and discuss which author they would like to write to. Remind them of the work they did on researching different authors and ask them to agree on one author the partners will write to. Encourage them to make notes of what they like about the author's work; which books they have read and any questions they want to ask.	
	### Plenary Remind the children about the formal and informal tone of letters. Ask them to suggest the tone their letters should have.	

DAY 2 ■ Drafting a letter

Key features	Stages	Additional opportunities
	### Introduction Display the letter begun yesterday. Continue to demonstrate how to write the letter. Check the layout with the class, such as: *Is my address in the correct place? Have I written the date?* Refer to the notes that you grouped into paragraphs and discuss how to order the paragraphs in the letter, for example, ask: *If this is a new topic, should I begin a new paragraph here?* Model writing the paragraphs, re-reading aloud to check the order makes sense and the letter flows well. Discuss how to end your letter and sign off. Read the finished letter aloud and orally demonstrate your thoughts by checking if you have repeated yourself, if the spelling is correct, and if the punctuation helps the letter make sense. Model how to re-draft some of the sections, and save a copy.	
Social skills: listen to and respect other people's ideas	### Independent work Ask the children to use the notes they made in pairs to draft their own letters. Tell them to read their draft letter aloud to their response partner and discuss the layout and the order of the paragraphs. Tell them to swap letters and check each other's for spelling and punctuation. Do all the questions end in a question mark? Have they spelled the author's name and book titles correctly?	**Support:** use photocopiable page 61 'Writing a letter' from Unit 3 to help them layout their letters
	### Plenary Ask the pairs to feed back about each other's letters and comment on two things that are good about them. Discuss the tone of the letters. Are they formal or informal, or a little of both? Ask the children to suggest why it is important that the name and book titles are all spelled correctly.	

DAY 3 ■ Polish a letter

Key features	Stages	Additional opportunities
	Introduction Display your finished letter and demonstrate how to give it a final check before printing off a copy. Explain that, if possible, you would like the children to send their letters to their chosen authors. Tell them to re-read and check their draft letters and then to write them as final polished versions.	
	Independent work Ask the children rewrite their drafts as finished letters. Some of the children could write their letters using word-processing software, others could write them by hand.	**Extend:** write their letters as emails and make comparisons with structure and style
Self-awareness: discuss and reflect on their personal responses to texts read	**Speaking and listening** Tell the children to swap their letters with a new response partner and ask them to read them aloud. The partners should check the layout, tone and content. Ask the children to make revisions based on their partner's feedback.	
Communication: communicate outcomes orally, in writing and through ICT	**Plenary** Ask the children to say which authors they have chosen to write to. Let those children who have chosen the same author read their letters aloud. Repeat with each author. Ask them to suggest what the author will say in response to their letters. Explain that it is possible that they might not get a response.	

DAY 4 ■ Letters for different purposes

Key features	Stages	Additional opportunities
Communication: appreciate the need to vary tone and content according to audience and purpose	**Introduction** Remind the children about the book reviews they wrote. Explain that you want them to choose a different book, and write a letter to a friend in the class to recommend the book to them. Discuss how a letter about a book might differ from a book review. Explain that the letter is to someone they know well and ask them to suggest how the tone of their letter will be different from the letter to an author, and from the tone of their book review. Choose a story and model how to write an informal letter to recommend this book to a friend. Demonstrate your thought processes aloud, for example: *What do I want to say about the book? Why ought my friend read it?* Demonstrate how to open a letter to a friend using an informal tone, and how choose to what you will say. Take suggestions from the class. Save a copy of your letter.	
Social skills: listen to and respect other people's opinions	**Speaking and listening** Ask the children to work with a partner and discuss which books they want to write about, and who they want to send their letter to.	
	Independent work Ask the children to make notes about their chosen book in order to encourage their friend to read it.	**Support:** some children could use their book reviews for information to put in their letters
	Plenary Ask some children to tell the class which book they have chosen and why.	

DAY 5 ■ A letter to a friend

Key features	Stages	Additional opportunities
Communication: appreciate the need to vary tone and content according to audience and purpose	**Introduction** Model how to complete the letter from yesterday's session. Read it with the class and ask them if it suits the purpose. *Will the friend want to read the book? Is the information in the letter interesting? Is the tone friendly and informal?* Ask the children to say how this letter differs from the class letter to Dick King-Smith.	**Support:** use photocopiable page 61 'Writing a letter' from Unit 3 to help them lay out their letters
	Independent work Ask the children to use their notes to write the letter to their friend.	
Communication: communicate outcomes orally	**Speaking and listening** Ask the children to 'send' their letter to the friend in the class. When they have read their letters from each other, ask them to feed back their response to it. *Was the letter easy to read? Did it make sense? Do they want to read the recommended book?*	
	Plenary Ask some of the recipients of letters to read them to the class, and some to describe how they enjoyed reading the letters. Did the letters achieve their purposes? Review the children's learning objectives with the class. Discuss which objectives have been achieved and what needs further work.	

Guided writing
Work with children during guided writing. Focus on using paragraphs for a change of subject and connectives to link paragraphs.

Assessment
Observe children's responses to letters received from friends. Have the letters been legible and clear? Did they achieve their purposes?
Do the children vary the tone of their writing to suit different audiences and purposes?
Ask the children to complete the CD-ROM assessment activity.
Refer back to the learning outcomes on page 67.

Further work
Encourage the children to write other letters for different purposes: to invite an author to visit the school, to recount an actual visit by a writer or story teller and so on.

Story summary

■ Find out before you start to write:

    1. Who is in the story (characters).

    2. What they say (plot).

    3. Where they are (setting).

The story extract is about _____

_____

_____

_____

The characters are _____

_____

_____

_____

_____

They talk about _____

_____

_____

_____

_____

The extract ends with _____

_____

_____

_____

_____

■ 100 LITERACY FRAMEWORK LESSONS YEAR 3

PHOTOCOPIABLE   ■SCHOLASTIC
www.scholastic.co.uk

The work of Dick King-Smith

■ Fill in the chart about the books you are reading. The first one has been done to help you.

Title	What are the settings?	Who is the main character?	What is the plot?	Who helps the main character?	What happens at the end?
Daggie Dogfoot	A farmyard. A pigsty. A river.	Daggie, a piglet.	Daggie wants to fly.	Geraldine, a duck.	Daggie becomes a great swimmer and rescues everyone from a flood.
A Mouse called Wolf					

Book review

Title:	A Mouse called Wolf
Author:	Dick King-Smith

What the book is about:

This book is about a very small mouse with a very big name – Wolfgang Amadeus Mouse – Wolf for short.

Wolf lives with his brothers and sisters in a house with a piano. The lady of the house, Mrs Honeybee, plays the piano everyday and Wolf loves to hear the music, but he gets teased by his brothers and sisters because he is so small.

When the brothers and sisters leave home, Wolf learns that he can sing! He becomes friends with Mrs Honeybee, but one day she falls down.

Wolf gets help by singing loudly at the window and when Mrs Honeybee is taken to hospital, Wolf really misses the music. So he makes up his own music to sing.

What I enjoyed about this book:

I liked the part where the cat became afraid of mice forever because it was funny. I think the idea of a singing mouse is funny and sweet at the same time, and the ending was really good, but you'll have to read it to find out why!

Who would enjoy this book:

Boys and girls will both like this book. Young children will enjoy listening to it, and children aged 8-12 will enjoy reading it.

Score:

I give this book 8/10 because I enjoyed it very much, but it wasn't as exciting as some of my favourite books.

By Sandy Thorne 3F

■ 100 LITERACY FRAMEWORK LESSONS YEAR 3

Book review writing frame

Title:

Author:

What the book is about:

What I enjoyed about this book:

Who would enjoy this book:

Score:

Traffic safety

■ Cut out the sections and rearrange them in the correct order.

14th January 2007

Mr J Goldie

Yours faithfully

The Chief Constable
Stafford

I would like you to take some action about this as soon as possible. It would help to slow the traffic if there were speed bumps in the road, and a crossing patrol to help the children cross safely. These measures are needed urgently to help the children stay safe.

Dear Sir

I am writing to draw your attention to a serious problem that affects the children of Maryfield School.

Maryfield School
School Lane
Bicford
Stafford
Midlands
S17 3GQ

I look forward to your speedy reply,

The speed of the cars makes it very dangerous. There have been three occasions where children were nearly knocked over. If this continues, there is bound to be a serious accident soon.

In recent months, the traffic around our school has grown. It has become almost impossible for the children to cross the road safely.

Headteacher

NARRATIVE
UNIT 5 Dialogue and plays

Speak and listen for a range of purposes on paper and on screen

Strand 1 Speaking
■ Sustain conversation, explain or give reasons for their views or choices.
Strand 3 Group discussion and interaction
■ Use discussion to organise roles and action.
■ Use the language of possibility to investigate and reflect on feelings, behaviour or relationships.
Strand 4 Drama
■ Present events and characters through dialogue to engage the interest of an audience.
■ Use some drama strategies to explore stories or issues.
■ Identify and discuss qualities of others' performances, including gestures, action and costume.

Read for a range of purposes on paper and on screen

Strand 7 Understanding and interpreting texts
■ Infer characters' feelings in fiction and consequences in logical explanations.
Strand 8 Engaging with and responding to texts
■ Share and compare reasons for reading preferences, extending range of books read.
■ Empathise with characters and debate moral dilemmas portrayed in texts.
■ Identify features that writers use to provoke readers' reactions.

Write for a range of purposes on paper and on screen

Strand 9 Creating and shaping texts
■ Make decisions about form and purpose, identify success criteria and use them to evaluate their own writing.
■ Select and use a range of technical and descriptive vocabulary.
■ Use layout, format, graphics and illustrations for different purposes.
Strand 10 Text structure and organisation
■ Signal sequence, place and time to give coherence.
Strand 11 Sentence structure and punctuation
■ Show relationships of time, reason and cause, through subordination and connectives.
■ Compose sentences using adjectives, verbs and nouns for precision, clarity and impact.
Strand 12 Presentation
■ Write with consistency in size and proportion of letters and spacing within and between words, using the correct formation of handwriting joins.
■ Develop accuracy and speed when using keyboard skills to type, edit and re-draft.

Progression in narrative

In this year children are moving towards:
■ Noting the use of language or music or camera angle to set scenes, build tension, create suspense; taking part in dramatised readings.
■ Understanding how settings are used to create atmosphere; looking at examples of scene changes that move the plot on, relieve or build up tension.

UNIT 5 ◄ Dialogue and plays continued

■ Including dialogue to set the scene and present characters; varying voice and intonation to create effects and sustain interest; exploring relationships and situations through drama.

Key aspects of learning covered in this Unit

Reasoning
Gather evidence to support ideas and give reasons.
Evaluation
Express their own views and preferences against agreed success criteria.
Empathy
Understand what others might be feeling in a particular situation.
Creative thinking
Use creative thinking to extend and consider alternatives to typical elements when writing and create dialogue of their own.
Social skills
When working collaboratively, children will listen and respect other people's ideas. They will take on different roles in a group.
Communication
Children will develop their ability to work collaboratively in paired, group and whole-class contexts. They will communicate outcomes orally, in writing and through ICT if appropriate.

Prior learning

Before starting this Unit check that the children can:
■ Understand the differences between a narrative story and a playscript.
■ Make a valid contribution to a collaborative group activity, listen to others and reach agreement within the group.
■ Differentiate between the speaker and the spoken words.
If they need further support please refer to a prior Unit or a similar Unit in Year 2.

Resources

Phase 1:
A moment in time 1 and 2 by Gill Friel ✎; *The three little pigs* by Gillian Howell ✎; *The three little pigs* (differentiated) by Gillian Howell ✎; Photocopiable page 97 'He said…'; Photocopiable page 98 'Speech marks'
Phase 2:
The three little pigs playscript by Gillian Howell ✎; Photocopiable page 99 'Playscript writing frame'; Photocopiable page 100 'Speech'
Phase 3:
Photocopiable page 99 'Playscript writing frame'; Zones of relevance board ✎; Familiar traditional tales and fairy stories; tape-recording equipment; Assessment activity 'Changing a story into a playscript' ✎

Cross-curricular opportunities

Drama and ICT

UNIT 5 ■ Teaching sequence

Phase	Children's objectives	Summary of activities	Learning outcomes
1	I can understand how dialogue affects plot.	Explore dialogue in a story and group role play.	Children can explain how the use and conventions of written dialogue differ between prose and playscripts.
		Explore another version of the story. Children choose verbs for dialogue in pairs.	
	I can identify characters and their dialogues.	Shared reading – choose other well-known stories and read only the dialogue.	
	I can understand how to punctuate dialogue.	Model writing a passage of dialogue. Punctuate a dialogue using speech marks.	
		Model writing a passage of dialogue. Punctuate a dialogue using speech marks.	
	I can tell a story through role play.	Shared reading – tell the story through role play in groups.	
2	I can understand the layout and features of a playscript.	Shared reading – role play the playscript.	Children can understand the conventions and features of playscript writing.
	I can learn about stage directions.	Shared activity focusing on stage directions. Annotate their own copies of the playscript.	
	I can continue a story through dialogue.	Shared writing – create a new scene. Plan dialogue in pairs.	
	I can write a new scene.	Shared writing – add stage directions. Annotate and write their own version.	
		Shared writing – add character details. Improve their own versions.	
3	I can understand which stories will make a good play.	Whole-class discussion. Plan a story to rewrite as a play. Vote on one story to rewrite.	Children can plan, write and perform a play based on a well-known story.
	I can plan a play.	Model writing a storyboard using The Three Billy Goats Gruff. Create their own storyboards.	
		Model writing scene one. Groups discuss plans and improvise dialogue.	
	I can write a playscript.	Model writing scene two. Write their play in groups.	
		Model writing scene three. Write their own scene in groups.	
	I can work out success criteria.	Revise playscript conventions and draw up success criteria. Write the ending of their plays.	
	I can add stage directions.	Model adding stage directions to The Three Billy Goats Gruff. Add stage directions to their playscripts.	
	I can rehearse and enhance the playscript.	Shared reading – The Three Billy Goats Gruff. Discuss sound effects for a radio play. Annotate own scripts.	
	I can evaluate writing.	Group rehearsals, performances and recording of radio plays.	

Provide copies of the objectives for the children.

DAY 1 ■ Voices

Key features	Stages	Additional opportunities
	### Introduction Explain that you are going to explore how dialogue is used in stories and in plays, and how it can be used to give more information and detail about the characters and the plot. Display *A moment in time 1* from the CD-ROM and read it with the children. Ask them to summarise orally what is happening in this extract. Ask the children to identify the spoken words and highlight them on the text. Ask the children to point out the punctuation that shows which parts are spoken by characters.	**MFW:** sure, year, friends, walk, walking, brother, younger
Creative thinking: extend and consider alternatives to open a story	### Speaking and listening Choose four children to read the dialogue aloud to the class, each taking a different character. When they have finished, discuss how much of the story can be inferred from the dialogue alone. Ask the children to find the reporting clauses in the text. Ask how the verbs *gasped, pleaded, laughed* affect the way the dialogue is spoken. Ask the children to describe the setting of the extract, and to suggest what might have happened before this point in the story. Ask them to think of what the characters might have said before they reached the ice. Sort the class into groups of four. Ask them to work out a role play using the four characters but adding conversation that occurs before the written extract.	**Performance:** use puppets to perform the role play
	### Plenary Ask some of the children to perform their role plays. Discuss how their spoken words conveyed thoughts, actions and events.	

DAY 2 ■ Alternative plots

Key features	Stages	Additional opportunities
	### Introduction Ask the children to tell you what happened in the extract they read in the previous session. Display *A moment in time 2* from the CD-ROM, having hidden or blocked out all the verbs used in the reporting clauses. Read the text together, using *said* to replace the hidden verbs, and ask the children to describe what is happening in the extract and how it differs from the shorter version. Highlight or underline all the spoken words and read the dialogue together. Ask the children to use expressive voices in order to convey the drama of the event. Go through the text again and ask the children to suggest verbs that could be used to describe the spoken words, based on their voices. Reveal the verbs in the reporting clauses one by one, and compare with the children's suggestions.	**MFW:** round, together, through
Social skills: listen to and respect other people's ideas		
Communication: collaborate when working in pairs	### Independent work Provide pairs of children with copies of photocopiable page 97 'He said...' and explain that this is a conversation between two people, but the verbs describing how they speak are missing. Ask them to read the dialogue together, each taking one character, and experiment with using different, expressive tones of voice. Ask them to choose verbs that best convey the expressions, first using verbs from the list and then verbs of their own, and fill in the missing verbs.	**Support:** choose from the selection of verbs at the bottom of the photocopiable sheet **Extend:** cover the box at the bottom of the photocopiable sheet and complete it using own choices
	### Plenary Ask some of the pairs to read their completed dialogues aloud. Discuss and compare their choices of verbs for the reporting clauses.	

DAY 3 ■ Dramatised reading

Key features	Stages	Additional opportunities

(handwritten: Wed day 3)

Introduction

Social skills: take on different roles in a group

Ask the children if they know the story of 'The three little pigs'. Encourage them to describe what happens in the story, or summarise it for them if necessary. Display *The three little pigs* from the CD-ROM. Read the extract from the story with the class, and ask them to describe the rest of the story orally. Choose children to take the roles of the characters and read the dialogue in the extract using expressive voices. Ask another four children to continue the story using their own dialogue and imaginations. Continue sections of the story so all the children are included.

MFW: round, brother, first, second, third

Support: read the differentiated text

Speaking and listening

Reasoning: gather evidence to support their ideas

Provide a selection of short, well-known stories for the children, for example traditional tales and fairy stories. Ask the children to work in groups and choose a story. Ask them to read the story together and identify the different characters. Ask them to divide the characters amongst the group and to read only the dialogue, using an expressive tone in role.

Performance: provide some groups with puppets for their role play

Plenary

Communication: communicate outcomes orally

Ask the groups of children to explain how they worked out who the characters were. Ask them how they identified the spoken words for each character. Allow enough time for each group to perform their role play for the class.

(handwritten: maybe this instead)

DAY 4 ■ Writing dialogue

Key features	Stages	Additional opportunities

Introduction

Communication: work collaboratively in whole-class contexts

Hold a short conversation with the class, for example, on how they came to school this morning. Ask the children to tell you what the conversation that you just had was about. Make up signs and sounds for different punctuation marks and repeat the conversation using them to show where the punctuation should be. Explain that you are going to write it together on the board. Write the first statement you made, for example *'Good morning everyone', said Mrs ...'* Ask the children to suggest what came next in the conversation and write it on the board, omitting the punctuation. Explain that a change of speaker needs a new line on which their words are written. Ask the children to help you correct your writing by adding the punctuation that denotes speech. Add one of their suggestions and place the reporting clause in the middle of the spoken words, and demonstrate how this affects the punctuation.

Support: complete the first paragraph only

Extend: type the passage using a computer

Independent work

Communication: communicate outcomes orally and in writing

Provide children with copies of photocopiable page 98 'Speech marks'. Ask them to read the passage aloud and then to add the missing punctuation that denotes the spoken words. Then let the children swap with a partner and read each other's punctuated dialogue, comparing it with their own.

Plenary

Ask the children to suggest reasons why punctuation is important and how it helped them to read the passage on the photocopiable sheet. Model how to punctuate the passage and children check their own against it.

(handwritten marginal notes near bottom right, illegible)

DAY 5 ■ Creating dialogue

wed
diff - Workshop
their own
conversation
+ punctuation ..

Key features	Stages	Additional opportunities
Creative thinking: extend and add new elements to a known story	**Introduction** Remind the children of how they continued the story of 'The three little pigs' in the whole-class session of Day 3. Ask the children to think about what happens when First Little Pig meets a man selling straw. Ask them to suggest what they say to each other. Encourage them to use their imaginations. Model writing their suggestions on the board, checking with the children about where to put speech marks and commas. Write some of their suggestions on the board without the punctuation and ask volunteers to come and add the correct punctuation marks.	
Communication: collaborate with a partner	**Independent work** Ask the children to work with a partner. Tell them to think about what the wolf and the three little pigs say when the wolf tries to blow down the last house. Tell them to write three sentences of the conversation and punctuate it. *wed m.*	**Extend:** let pairs of children write the conversation on a computer
	Plenary Ask the pairs to exchange their written conversations with a different pair and to read the swapped dialogue aloud. Discuss how easy or difficult it is to read with expression.	

DAY 6 ■ Acting the story

Key features	Stages	Additional opportunities
	Introduction Display *The three little pigs* from the CD-ROM. Read the extract and together, continue the story. Ask the children to say who the characters are and create a list. (There are eight characters in total in this version.) Explain that they are going to retell the story through role play. Ask the children to suggest if any parts of the story would be missed out if they told the story through the characters' voices. Do they need a narrator?	**Film:** watch an animated version of the story on video
Social skills: work collaboratively in a group, taking on different roles	**Speaking and listening** Ask the children to work in groups, allocate a chairperson and plan how they could tell the story through role play. Encourage the children to allocate roles and plan the dialogue. Ask them to think if they need to make notes. Let them rehearse the story before performing it.	**Role play:** use small-world play equipment and toys to recreate the story; create masks for the characters during art lessons
Communication: communicate outcomes orally	**Plenary** Allow sufficient time for each of the groups to perform their role play for the class. Discuss and compare the role plays. Ask the groups how they planned what the dialogue should be and how closely they stuck to their plans. Did some of the groups improvise their conversations?	**Support:** give the group a reduced number of characters

Guided reading
During guided reading, identify dialogue and the conventions for writing and punctuation.

Assessment
Paired assessment: Are children able to read and understand punctuated dialogue? Are they able to correct an unpunctuated piece of dialogue? Refer back to the learning outcomes on page 85.

Further work
Provide pieces of badly punctuated dialogue for children to correct. Hold conversations orally using signs and sounds to show the punctuation.

DAY 1 ■ Playscripts

Key features	Stages	Additional opportunities
Reasoning: gather evidence to support ideas	**Introduction** Remind the class about the extract they read of *The three little pigs* and their group role plays. Mask and hide all the words in italic print inside brackets before displaying the playscript version of the story from the CD-ROM. Ask the class to suggest how this is similar to and different from the first extract. Explain that this is a script for a play. Discuss how the purpose and audience of a playscript differs from a written story, for example it tells a cast of characters what to say, and the intended audience is the cast. The final audience is 'watchers' or 'listeners' rather than 'readers'. Point out the words *Scene 1* and ask the children to say what they think this means and its purpose. Discuss the layout and features of the text. Point out and read the cast list together. Ask the children to read the left hand column of characters who feature in this scene, then read the spoken parts of the playscript·together.	
Social skills: take on different roles when working in a group	**Speaking and listening** Provide the children with printed copies (with hidden italics) and ask the children to work in groups of four. Tell them to take a character each and to read the script, then to swap roles and re-read it.	**Support:** let children swap roles only once
	Plenary Ask the children to describe the purpose of a playscript. Ask some of the groups to read the script aloud. Ask the class to suggest where scene 2 might be set.	

DAY 2 ■ Stage directions

Key features	Stages	Additional opportunities
Reasoning: use evidence from texts to explain their differences	**Introduction** Remind the class about their reading of the playscript in the previous session. Ask them to say what the main differences were between the script and the story. Elicit that the story had more details that describe events and characters, and the script only told readers what the characters said. Display the playscript and reveal the italicised stage directions. Ask the children to read them and to suggest their purpose in the script. Explain that the italic words are written to give the characters some information about how to say some of their words and where to go on the stage. Ask the children to suggest a reason why these words are written in a different style of print, such as to differentiate them from the 'spoken' part of the script.	
Social skills: listen to and respect other people's ideas	**Speaking and listening** Ask the children to work in groups of four and read the script using expressive voices. Ask them to suggest other stage directions they think would help them interpret the script in a more lively way. Ask them to think how to ensure their stage directions are not mistaken for dialogue, for example a different colour or writing style.	**Support:** work with a group who need support, scribing their ideas
	Independent work Ask the children to annotate their copies of the script to add stage directions.	
	Plenary Discuss and compare the children's additions to the stage directions.	

DAY 3 ■ A new scene

Key features	Stages	Additional opportunities
Creative thinking: extend and consider alternative conversations between two characters	### Introduction Display the playscript. Ask the children to re-read the spoken words and describe how written dialogue in a script is different from dialogue in a story (no use of speech marks, no reporting clauses, the speaker is listed on the left side of the page each time they speak). Re-read the cast of characters and ask the children to identify which characters feature in scene 1. Ask them to suggest what might happen in scene 2 and which characters feature in it. *Does Mrs Porker feature? Do all three little pigs feature?* Explain that you are going to write scene 2 where First Little Pig meets the man carrying straw. Ask the children to suggest where the scene should be set. Model how to write the scene and the setting using the conventions of playscript writing. Write the first character and a line of dialogue, thinking aloud and editing/altering your words. Ask the children for suggestions of dialogue between the two characters. Scribe their ideas, checking the spelling and punctuation with the children as you write. ### Independent work Ask the children to work with a partner and to plan the dialogue for scene 2 orally first and then on paper. Ask them to work with another pair of children and describe their ideas. ### Plenary Ask some of them to role play their scenes. Discuss and compare the children's ideas.	**Support:** use photocopiable page 99 'Playscript writing frame' to help them use the correct layout for a playscript

DAY 4 ■ Adding stage directions

Key features	Stages	Additional opportunities
Creative thinking: use creative thinking to extend and consider alternatives to their playscript annotations **Social skills:** listen to and respect other people's ideas	### Introduction Display an enlarged copy of one of the children's plans for scene 2 on the board. Discuss where the scene is set and model how to write this on the script as a stage direction. Read the script with the class using expressive voices. Ask the children to suggest adverbs that could tell the cast about how to say the dialogue. Add some of their suggestions to the board. ### Speaking and listening Ask the children to work with their response partner and read their planned dialogue from yesterday's session. Tell them to use expressive voices. Ask the partners to suggest adverbs that describe the words or suggest how the words should be said. Encourage them to annotate their plans to add these as stage directions. Ask them to discuss any movements of actions the characters take. Discuss whether direction would be needed for a cast and add them to the plans as appropriate. ### Independent work Ask the children to begin writing their plans as a more polished scene. ### Plenary Ask some of the pairs to read their scripts aloud, including any new stage directions. Ask the others to compare with their own to see if they could be improved by adding or deleting stage directions.	**Support:** annotate photocopiable page 99 'Playscript writing frame' to help them maintain the correct layout for a playscript **Extend:** ask the children to write their playscripts using ICT

DAY 5 ■ Polish and performance

Key features	Stages	Additional opportunities
Self-awareness: discuss and reflect on their personal responses to texts read	**Introduction** Explain to the children that today they are going to finish writing scene 2 for a play about 'The three little pigs'. Display the playscript of *The three little pigs* from the CD-ROM. Ask the class to read the script and focus on the dialogue spoken by the characters. Ask them to suggest what sort of personalities Mrs Porker and each of the Little Pigs has. Explain that, in a playscript, the character and feelings of the cast has to be described through their spoken words, unlike in a narrative story when the author can write descriptive sentences or paragraphs. Ask the children to suggest words or phrases spoken by Mrs Porker that give clues to her personality and annotate the playscript. Ask them if the dialogue tells them anything about the personalities of the Little Pigs. Elicit that each is looking for something different in their new homes – *pretty, warm, strong*.	
	Independent work Ask the children to re-read their new scenes and add or alter any dialogue to give their audience some clues about the first little pig and about the man with the straw.	**Extend:** edit scenes using ICT
Communication: communicate outcomes orally	**Plenary** Ask some pairs of children to read the first scene and their new scene aloud for the class. Discuss and compare the effectiveness of their scripts. Review the children's learning targets for this Unit and discuss areas for improvement and further work.	

Guided writing
Work with groups during guided writing to explore the effect of different types of stage directions and annotations to their new play scenes.

Assessment
Peer assessment: Are pairs of children able to read and understand each other's newly devised scenes?
Observation: Do the children maintain the structure and layout of a playscript?
Do the children choose adverbs to describe spoken words?
Do the children contribute to role play when reading their scenes aloud?
Refer back to the learning outcomes on page 85.

Further work
Let the children rewrite their scenes on a word processor or using presentation software.
Use photocopiable page 100 'Speech' to give children extra practise in using accurate adverbs to describe speech.

DAY 1 ■ Making story choices

Key features	Stages	Additional opportunities
Reasoning: gather evidence to support their opinions about books and giving reasons **Social skills:** listen to and respect other people's opinions	**Introduction** Explain to the class that they are going to be writing a play based on a familiar story and then performing it in groups for the class and recording them for other classes to listen to. Provide the children with a selection of familiar traditional tales and fairy stories. Together, select some of the titles and discuss which ones could be rewritten as a play. Display the Zones of relevance board from the CD-ROM and write some of the children's suggestions in the appropriate bands, for example the number of characters needed for the cast in some stories. Tell them to think about the number of group members. Ask them to consider the settings of different stories and how often the scenes would need to change. Experiment with different stories grouped in order of suitability. **Speaking and listening** Invite the children to work in groups and to choose no more than three stories to consider. Ask them to discuss and consider how easy or difficult it would be to rewrite them as a playscript. Tell them to agree on one story for their own group. **Plenary** Ask a representative from each of the groups to describe the story they have chosen and why they feel it would be an appropriate one to use as a play. Discuss and compare the groups' choices and hold a show of hands for each story. Select the two most popular titles and hold a class vote. Explain that their final choice will be used as the basis for all the groups' plays.	limit the children's choices if preferred, to titles that you wish them to choose from that have an appropriate number of characters

DAY 2 ■ Storyboard

Key features	Stages	Additional opportunities
Communication: work collaboratively in a group **Social skills:** listen to and respect other people's ideas	**Introduction** Explain that you are going to be using 'The Three Billy Goats Gruff' as a model for writing a play, and demonstrate how to begin planning a playscript. Tell an oral version of the story to the class, and model how to create a storyboard to show the plot, for example: 1) three goats are tired of their own grass and decide to cross the river; 2) Little BG and Middle BG each meet the troll; 3) Big BG tosses the troll into the river; 4) three goats eat fresh new grass. Draw an outline plan by first writing the names of the characters in a list. Ask the children to suggest how many different settings are needed. Ask them to recall how the setting is written and described in a playscript. Keep a copy. **Speaking and listening** Encourage the children to work in their groups and collaborate on drawing a storyboard to describe the plot of the story chosen in yesterday's plenary vote. Tell them to use notes and write the plot as briefly as possible. Remind them that this is to help them plan the play and not intended to be the script. Ask them to decide on who the characters will be and to write a cast list. **Plenary** Ask some of the groups to show and describe their storyboards to the class. Discuss and compare their differences.	**Support:** provide children with sentence starters

DAY 3 ■ Scene 1

Key features	Stages	Additional opportunities
Creative thinking: consider alternatives for characters' lines **Social skills:** take on different roles in a group	**Introduction** Display the storyboard for 'The Three Billy Goats Gruff' created yesterday. Explain that you are going to work out the scenes today and begin writing scene 1. Discuss how many scenes there should be, based on your storyboard outline. Model how to make notes showing what should be the setting for each scene. Ask the children to read the cast list and suggest which characters feature in each scene. Add them to your storyboard. Explain that now you have an outline of 'Who' and 'Where' you are going to begin working on the characters' lines, and explain that this is the term used to describe the spoken words in a script. Ask the children to suggest who should speak first and what they will say. Model how to write the first character and his lines. Keep a copy. **Speaking and listening** Ask the groups of children to collaborate in deciding how many scenes should be in the play. Tell them to annotate their storyboard, making notes of where each scene is set and which characters feature in them. Let them allocate the characters' roles and orally improvise their dialogue. **Independent work** Ask the children to begin writing their own copy of the play, writing the title, the cast list and beginning scene 1. **Plenary** Ask some of the groups to read their opening dialogue.	**Support:** let children use an adapted copy of photocopiable page 99 'Playscript writing frame' to help them write the dialogue

DAY 4 ■ Scene 2

Key features	Stages	Additional opportunities
Creative thinking: extend and consider alternatives for dialogue in a playscript **Communication:** work collaboratively in a group context **Evaluation:** express their own views and preferences	**Introduction** Remind the children of how they devised scene 1. Discuss scene 2 with the class and model how to show the change of scene in a playscript. Discuss which characters are going to be in this scene, such as Little and Middle Billy Goats and the Troll. Use shared writing to continue the dialogue for scene 2. Encourage the children to experiment with the characters' lines to add interest to the play. **Speaking and listening** Ask the groups of children to share the dialogue they wrote for scene 1 with each other. Ask them to choose one of their playscripts, allocate roles and read through the script aloud. They should then discuss what the characters will say in scene 2. **Independent work** Ask the groups to continue writing their own playscripts to show the change of scene and adding the new lines for each character. **Plenary** Choose one group to read their first scene and a different group to read their second scene. Ask the children to comment on the characters' lines and make suggestions for improvement and to add interest.	**Support:** use an adapted copy of photocopiable page 99 'Playscript writing frame' to help write the dialogue

DAY 5 ■ Scene 3

Key features	Stages	Additional opportunities
Communication: collaborate with others in whole-class contexts	**Introduction** Display the collaborative class playscript. Explain to the children that you are now going to write the third scene, where the play reaches its climax – the most exciting part of the story where Big Billy Goat Gruff meets the Troll. Ask the children to suggest what they will say to each other, what the other two Billy Goats are doing and if they are in this scene. Do the two Billy Goats have any lines? Ask the class for suggestions and model writing their lines on the playscript. **Speaking and listening** Ask the groups to refer to their storyboards and decide on the content of the third scene for their playscript. Tell them to improvise the characters' lines to suit the scene.	
Social skills: listen to and respect other people's ideas	**Independent work** Ask the children to continue writing the next scene on their group copies of the playscript. Ask the groups to reform and discuss what each of them has added to their playscripts. Ask them to each read their script aloud to the group and discuss how their plays should end. **Plenary** Take feedback from the class, Discuss and compare their choices for an ending to their plays.	**Extend:** children who have worked at an advanced pace begin writing their scripts using ICT

DAY 6 ■ Success criteria

Key features	Stages	Additional opportunities
Evaluation: discuss success criteria for their written work	**Introduction** Tell the children that a playscript is another way of writing a story and remind them of the typical elements of writing a story, for example an opening, a problem, a build up to a resolution and ending. Ask the children what is required when writing a story as a play. Take suggestions and write them on the board. Encourage the children to think about the layout and conventions of playscripts, how dialogue can move the plot forward, how to include setting or character description, stage directions, sentence construction and punctuation. Discuss the elements on the board and rewrite them as a list of children's targets for success. Explain that they will be using this list as an aid to evaluating their group playscripts at the end of the Unit. Keep a copy. **Independent work** Ask the children to write the ending to their group copies of the playscripts.	
Evaluation: give feedback to others	**Speaking and listening** Ask the children to swap their playscripts with other groups. Tell them to read each other's script and compare and comment on the plays.	**Extend:** ask the children to finish their scripts using ICT
Social skills: listen to and respect other people's ideas	**Plenary** Ask some of the children to feed back their responses to the playscripts. Discuss what else is needed to improve and polish them. Will it be easy for a cast of actors to read and interpret?	

DAY 7 ▪ Adding stage directions

Key features	Stages	Additional opportunities
Communication: collaborate with others in whole-class contexts **Empathy:** understand what others might be feeling in a particular situation	**Introduction** Display 'The Three Billy Goats Gruff' playscript. Allocate the roles and ask the children to read their respective lines aloud. Discuss the characters. Ask the children to suggest if their lines are realistic. Do they sound like something they would say if they actually were that character? Amend and improve the spoken words from the children's responses. Remind the children about adding stage directions to inform the actors about your intentions as authors. Ask the children to suggest what stage directions they should add to this script and use shared writing to demonstrate where and how to write their suggestions. **Speaking and listening** Encourage the children to work in their groups and collaborate to read their scripts aloud. Tell them to use expressive voices and add stage directions that are needed to describe how lines should be spoken. Ask them to add stage directions to tell actors when and where to move.	
Social skills: take on different roles in a group	**Independent work** Ask the children to add stage directions to their group copies of the scripts and make any alterations to bring them to completion. **Plenary** Invite children who altered any dialogue in their scripts to describe the changes and say how it has improved the dialogue. Discuss how the group plays should be performed.	**ICT:** let children use ICT to polish their playscripts

DAY 8 ▪ Rehearsals

Key features	Stages	Additional opportunities
Creative thinking: extend and consider alternatives to enhance performance of their plays	**Introduction** Remind the children of the discussion about performing their group plays in yesterday's plenary session. Tell the children about the intention to record the performances so that other children in the school can listen to them. Ask the children to suggest an occasion when a play is heard but not seen. Elicit the response 'on the radio'. Using 'The Three Billy Goats Gruff' as a model, allocate the roles to different children and ask them to read the play aloud while the rest of the class close their eyes. Discuss the effect and ask the children to suggest if sound effects would enhance their appreciation of the play, for example should there be a sound-effect to show the sound that the Billy Goats make on the wooden bridge?	
	Speaking and listening Ask the groups to discuss their scripts and decide if any sound effects are needed. Ask them to consider and suggest any equipment they could use to create the sound effects. They should annotate their texts using stage direction conventions accordingly. **Plenary** Take feedback from the groups about their ideas for sound effects. Praise good ideas and allow other groups to borrow them. Ask some of the children to read their playscripts aloud to the class. Collect them and display them as a class book of plays.	**ICT:** polish the group script using ICT and print copies for each group member

DAY 9 ■ Performance and evaluation

Key features	Stages	Additional opportunities
	Introduction Explain that each group will be performing the play and recording it using audio tape.	
Social skills: take on different roles in a group	**Speaking and listening** Allow each group time to practise and rehearse their plays, using any sound effects thought of in the previous session. Ask each group to allocate a member to announce the name of their play and the names of the actors who are performing it, then to perform and record their plays. When they are all completed, play the recordings to the class.	
Evaluation: express their views and preferences against agreed criteria to evaluate the work of others	**Independent work** Discuss the success criteria drawn up on Day 6. Ask the groups to swap their script with another group, read and evaluate it based on the success criteria. Ask the children to evaluate their own group playscript and performance.	
	Plenary Discuss the audio recordings the class listened to. Ask the children to express their preferences with supporting reasons for them. Take feedback from the group evaluations of their own and other groups' playscripts. Ask them to say if a different group would be able to act the play as effectively as the group who wrote it and give reasons for their opinions.	**Extend:** make the completed audio recordings available for other children to listen to

Guided writing

In guided writing, work with groups to use the conventions of playscript writing. Encourage the use of adverbials for stage directions.

In guided reading, select a playscript at an appropriate level for the group and read it together, taking different characters' parts.

Assessment

Observation: Do the children collaborate and agree roles in group work?

Peer assessment: Do the children give reasoned responses to other people's writing, with evidence to support their opinions?

Ask the children to complete the assessment activity on the CD-ROM 'Changing a story into a playscript'. Refer back to the learning outcomes on page 85.

Further work

Ask the children to read and perform other published plays in group work, such as *Play Time* by Julia Donaldson. Encourage the children to use other well-known stories as a basis for writing a play.

Name _____ Date _____

He said...

■ Fill in the missing verbs to describe the spoken words.

"Look at all the snow!" _____ Finn as he drew back his bedroom curtains.

"Everything is white," _____ his brother Angus.

"Let's go and build a snowman," _____ Finn.

"Okay, but first you're going to look at the river with me," _____ Angus.

"No, let's make a snowman first," _____ Finn.

"Don't be so bossy!" _____ Angus, "I want to see if it's frozen. I want to slide on the ice."

whispered	**gasped**	**cried**	**suggested**
demanded	**argued**	**pleaded**	
laughed	**urged**	**shouted**	

Speech marks

■ Add speech marks to the passages to show what the characters said.

Soon Second Little Pig met a woodcutter.

Hello Mr Woodcutter, said Second Little Pig, you have got a great big pile of sticks there. Can you spare some for me?

Certainly. What do you want sticks for? asked the woodcutter.

I am going to build a lovely warm house to live in boasted Second Little Pig.

Later, Third Little Pig met a man who was making bricks.

Hello Mr Brick-maker said Third Little Pig.

Hello Little Pig, answered the brick-maker, where are you off to today?

I am going to build a good strong house to live in. Will you let me have some of your bricks?

That's a good idea said the brick-maker. Bricks make strong houses, he added.

■ 100 LITERACY FRAMEWORK LESSONS YEAR 3

PHOTOCOPIABLE ■SCHOLASTIC
www.scholastic.co.uk

Playscript writing frame

Scene 2

Write the name of each speaker here.	Write how they speak here.	Write the spoken words here.
First Little Pig	*(very loudly)*	Hello kind Sir. What a lot of straw you have got!

Speech

■ Choose the adverb to describe the spoken words from the choices on the right of the page.

"Come back at once!"	he said _____	loudly
		loud

"Oh no! The Wolf is here,"	he said _____	fearfully
		fearful

"I haven't a moment to spare,"	she said _____	hurriedly
		hurried

"I'm not crying really,"	he said _____	sad
		sadly

"This is wonderful!"	they said _____	happy
		happily

"This is exactly what you do,"	he said _____	slowly
		slow

■ 100 LITERACY FRAMEWORK LESSONS YEAR 3

NON-FICTION
UNIT 1 Reports

Speak and listen for a range of purposes on paper and on screen

Strand 1 Speaking
- Explain process or present information, ensuring items are clearly sequenced, relevant details are included and accounts ended effectively.

Strand 2 Listening and responding
- Identify the presentational features used to communicate the main points in a broadcast.
- Identify key sections in an information broadcast, noting how the language used signals changes or transitions in focus.

Read for a range of purposes on paper and on screen

Strand 7 Understanding and interpreting texts
- Identify and make notes on the main points of section(s) of text.
- Identify how different texts are organised, including reference texts, magazines and leaflets, on paper and on screen.

Strand 8 Engaging and responding to texts
- Identify features that writers use to provoke readers' reactions.

Write for a range of purposes on paper and on screen

Strand 9 Creating and shaping texts
- Write non-narrative texts using structures of different text-types.
- Select and use a range of technical and descriptive vocabulary.
- Use layout, format, graphics and illustrations for different purposes.

Strand 10 Text structure and organisation
- Signal sequence, place and time to give coherence.
- Group related material into paragraphs.

Strand 11 Sentence structure and punctuation
- Show relationships of time, reason and cause through subordination and connectives.
- Compose sentences using adjectives, verbs and nouns for precision, clarity and impact.
- Clarify meaning through the use of exclamation marks and speech marks.

Strand 12 Presentation
- Write with consistency in size and proportion of letters and spacing within and between words, using the correct formation of handwriting joins.

Progression in non-chronological reports

In this year children are moving towards:
- Analysing a number of report texts and noting their function, form and typical language features.
- Distinguishing between generalisations and specific information and between recounts and reports, using content taken from another area of the curriculum.
- Analysing broadcast information to identify presentation techniques and noticing how the language used signals change.
- Writing own report independently based on notes from several sources.

▶

UNIT 1 ◄ Reports *continued*

Key aspects of learning covered in this Unit

Enquiry
Children will ask questions arising from work in another area of the curriculum, for example on teeth and eating, research and then plan how to present the information effectively.

Information processing
Children will identify relevant information from a range of sources on paper and on screen and use this to write their own non-chronological reports.

Evaluation
Children will present information orally and in writing. They will discuss success criteria, give feedback to others and judge the effectiveness of their own work.

Social skills
When developing collaborative writing, children will learn to listen to and respect others' viewpoints and take on different roles within a group to complete a task.

Communication
Children will develop their ability to discuss the content and presentation of the reports they are listening to, reading and writing. They will often work collaboratively in pairs and groups. They will communicate outcomes orally, in writing and through ICT.

Prior learning

Before starting this Unit check that the children can:
■ Write three facts about something that interests them in three sentences, using capital letters and full stops (and commas for lists, if appropriate), consistently using the present tense and precise vocabulary.
■ Explain organisational features of texts, including alphabetical order, layout, diagrams, captions, hyperlinks and bullet points.
■ If this is the first Unit in the year, read and spell a range of common words, all digraphs and trigraphs, numbers to twenty, days, months, colours and words ending in suffixes *-ful* and *-ly*.
If they need further support please refer to a prior Unit or a similar Unit in Year 2.

Resources

Phase 1:
Dinosaurs – when and where by James Friel ✤; *Dinosaurs – sizes and shapes* by James Friel ✤; Photocopiable page 117 'KWL Chart: Dinosaurs'; Non-chronological report skeleton ✤; Range of non-fiction books ideally on birds and dinosaurs

Phase 2:
'Endangered species: Polar Bears' video ✤; Endangered species wildlife film

Phase 3:
Birds by Gill Friel ✤; *Birdwatcher's guide* by Gill Friel ✤; Photocopiable page 118 'Reports'; Photocopiable page 119 'Robin'; Non-chronological report skeleton ✤; Range of non-fiction books ideally on birds and dinosaurs

Phase 4:
Photocopiable page 120 'Report writing frame'; Non-chronological report skeleton ✤; Range of non-fiction books; Assessment activity 'Non-chronological reports' ✤

Cross-curricular opportunities

Science

UNIT 1 ■ Teaching sequence

Phase	Children's objectives	Summary of activities	Learning outcomes
1	I can understand the difference between fiction and non-fiction.	Explore a range of different text-types. Group discussion.	Children can find a key word using an index and then locate the relevant information on a page.
	I can make notes.	Explore a non-fiction text, establishing prior knowledge. Paired activity note making.	Children demonstrate that they have understood information read from a book or screen by noting the main points.
	I can identify key ideas in paragraphs.	Annotate a non-chronological report.	
	I can write notes as a list.	Identify main points and write notes as a list.	
	I can identify key facts.		
	I can use a graphic organiser.	Shared writing using a report skeleton. Make notes on their own skeletons.	
2	I can watch and listen.	Watch a film or television programme. Teacher demonstrates note-making. Children write a sentence as a summary.	Children can use clear language and presentational features observed on a broadcast to make their own oral presentation interesting.
		Watch the video from the CD-ROM. Make comparisons and make notes.	
	I can make an oral presentation.	Whole-class discussion about making an oral presentation. Plan and make group presentations.	
	I can agree success criteria.		
3	I can locate information.	Model reading to find information using contents and index. Read in pairs and write questions.	Children can recognise the structure and language features of a non-chronological report.
	I can write a paragraph.	Model reading to identify features and grammatical structure. Rewrite text as a paragraph.	
	I can know when to use captions and labels.	Model reading to identify key points. Write captions and labels.	
4	I can contribute information.	Shared writing using a skeleton to plan a report.	Children note information collected from reading more than one source and present it in the form of a non-chronological report.
	I can use headings and subheadings.	Model writing using skeleton notes on a writing frame. Brainstorm headings and subheadings.	
	I can use paragraphing.	Model writing, adding complete sentences. Write own sentences and discuss.	
	I can use a writing frame.	Shared writing to complete the writing frame. Write draft reports.	
	I can research information.	Research and make notes for a class encyclopedia.	
	I can write paragraphs.	Write drafts using a writing frame.	
	I can finish a report.	Polish a draft as a finished page for the class encyclopedia.	

Provide copies of the objectives for the children.

DAY 1 ■ Types of text

Key features	Stages	Additional opportunities
	## Introduction
Explain to the children that they are going to be exploring a range of different types of non-fiction texts, and working towards researching and writing their own non-fiction reports. Ask the children to suggest the key differences between fiction and non-fiction. Ask them also to name any types of non-fiction texts they know from previous work and their own experience. Encourage them to use terms such as: *encyclopedia, instructions, recipes, how-to books, explanations* and *reports*. Explain that in this Unit the focus of work will be on non-chronological reports. Ask them to suggest a meaning for the term *non-chronological* and define it for them if necessary. Provide a range of non-fiction books of different text types if possible on the topics of birds and of dinosaurs for the class to explore. Ask the children to explore the available books and decide if they are instructions, non-chronological reports, explanations or alphabetically-ordered texts.	**Extend:** groups could use the internet or CD-ROM non-fiction texts
Communication: develop their ability to discuss the content and presentation of reports	## Speaking and listening
Give the children, in groups, a selection of varied non-fiction books. Ask them to look briefly at the books, including the title, the layout and the back cover blurb, discuss what type of text it is and use Post-it Notes to label what type of text they think each one is.

Plenary
Take feedback from each group. Ask them to describe one or two books and what type of text it is. Ask them to give a reason for their opinion. | **Support:** provide a poster, or write on the board, the typical key features of each text type for reference |

DAY 2 ■ Dinosaur report

Key features	Stages	Additional opportunities
Communication: discuss the content and presentation of reports; work collaboratively in pairs; communicate outcomes orally	## Introduction
Display *Dinosaurs – when and where* from the CD-ROM. Read the title and ask the class to suggest what sort of text this is, for example: is it a story or will it give them information? Elicit that it is a non-fiction text. Ask the children to give reasons for their answers. Re-read the title and ask them to suggest what sort of information they will find in the text. Discuss what the children already know about the subject and draw up a list on the board.
Model how to make brief notes rather than writing in full sentences.

Speaking and listening
Give children ten minutes and ask them in pairs or groups to tell each other everything they know about dinosaurs already, for example from reading and from watching film and television. | **MFW:** today, animals, years, around, first, earth, together |
| **Enquiry:** ask questions | ## Independent work
Ask the children to work with a partner and use photocopiable page 117 'KWL Chart: Dinosaurs' to make notes about what they already know, and what they want to know, about when and where dinosaurs lived. Ensure that they focus on *when* and *where* only. Ask them to keep the chart for use in a later session.

Plenary
Let some of the children explain what they already know by referring to the notes they made. Ask children to say what they want to know and compare their responses. Ask them to suggest how they can find the answers. | **Support:** work with pairs of children to support them reading and identifying the main points |

DAY 3 ■ Annotating texts

Key features	Stages	Additional opportunities
Information processing: identify relevant information	**Introduction** Display the text *Dinosaurs – when and where* from the CD-ROM. Read the text to the children, and ask them to suggest the specific text type. Eliminate certain types of text by asking: *Is this a set of instructions? Is this an encyclopedia?* and so on. Explain that you are going to re-read the text together and identify words and phrases that tell you that it is a non-chronological report. Using the highlighter or pen and different colours, mark the vocabulary and discuss it with the children, for example general rather than specific participants *everyone, dinosaurs, humans, scientists, people.* Ask the children to identify the paragraphs.	
Communication: work collaboratively in pairs; communicate outcomes orally and in writing	**Speaking and listening** Ask the children to work with a partner. Encourage them to suggest the main point or purpose of the text, and the key ideas of each paragraph. **Independent work** Provide the children with copies of the text and ask them to annotate their copies to show one key idea for each paragraph, plus any general plural nouns, and connectives used to link ideas, sentences and paragraphs.	**Extend:** group the connectives in the text according to time and cause
	Plenary Ask some of the children to describe the key ideas of each of the paragraphs. Invite other children to identify connectives.	

DAY 4 ■ Note making

Key features	Stages	Additional opportunities
Information processing: identify relevant information	**Introduction** Display the text *Dinosaurs – when and where* from the CD-ROM. Explain that you are going to use the children's findings and notes made yesterday to annotate the text and identify the main points. Re-read the text, and model how to underline the main facts as you are reading, for example *died out 65 million years ago*, stopping and discussing your choices with the class. Print a copy of the annotated text, and explain that you are going to begin to write a list of the main facts for use in future writing. Demonstrate how to write brief notes on the board, using incomplete sentences and abbreviations, for example *d. 65m yrs*. Ask the children to suggest the reason for using brief notes rather than writing in full sentences. Ask them to suggest how to abbreviate words, such as missing out letters and using initials.	
Communication: work collaboratively in pairs	**Independent work** Ask the children to work with their partners again, and to underline all the main facts on their copies of the text, and then, by referring to their annotated texts, to write the main facts as a list of brief notes.	**Support:** provide a glossary of possible abbreviations
	Plenary Invite the children to describe what they have learned by reading and annotating the text. Remind the children of their KWL charts. Encourage them to add anything they have learned in the final column.	

DAY 5 ■ Three key facts

Key features	Stages	Additional opportunities
Information processing: identify relevant information **Enquiry:** research information	**Introduction** Explain that you are going to look at more information about dinosaurs using a different text. Display *Dinosaurs – sizes and shapes* from the CD-ROM. Ask the children to read the title. Discuss what information they think they will find in the text, such as what dinosaurs looked like. Read the text together. Ask the children to identify any specific dinosaur names and highlight them in the text. Explain to the children that you want them to read the text with their partner and find three facts about the appearance of the dinosaurs referred to in the text. **Speaking and listening** Provide the children with a copy of the text. Encourage the children to re-read the text with their partner and to discuss the main points made about each dinosaur. Ask them to decide on three important pieces of information about each one and mark them on their copies. **Independent work** Ask the children to write their annotations as a list of notes for use in future writing. **Plenary** Name each dinosaur one at a time and ask different children to state a fact about its appearance that they have learned by reading the text. Discuss and compare the facts they identified as being important, and ask them which three facts they used in their notes and why they chose them.	**Support:** provide a glossary of abbreviations

DAY 6 ■ Dinosaur skeleton

Key features	Stages	Additional opportunities
Enquiry: plan how to present information	**Introduction** Discuss the methods of finding and noting information that the children have used in this Unit. Explain that, if they were to use this information to write their own non-chronological reports about dinosaurs, they would need to make a plan showing how they would group the facts they want to include. Discuss the possible content of the report and make a list of headings, such as *When they lived*; *What different sorts*; *What happened to them*. Explain that you are going to use a graphic organiser to put all the different pieces of information into one place, according to the headings. Display the Non-chronological report skeleton from the CD-ROM. Explain that this organiser allows you to write notes for all the different areas of the topic and add any further information. Using the headings as topic areas, demonstrate how to write them on the skeleton. Ask the children for some of their facts and model how to note them around each heading. Discuss the heading *Different sorts of dinosaur* and list the relevant facts around the heading. **Independent work** Provide the children with blank copies of the skeleton and ask them to organise their key facts around the names of the dinosaurs. **Plenary** Ask some children to read their notes for each of the dinosaurs.	**Extend:** research further information using websites such as http://news.bbc.co.uk/cbbcnews/hi/guides/default.stm

Guided reading

Select a text at an appropriate level for the group. Support the children as they read. Discuss the way the information is presented, for example how do illustrations, charts and photographs help them understand the information? Discuss the structure of the text, locate and use contents and index pages. Examine the use of paragraphs and identify their key ideas.

Identify and list new vocabulary.

Assessment

Observation: Are the children able to differentiate between fiction and non-fiction?

Can the children skim-read and scan a text to locate relevant information?

Do the children use brief notes and abbreviations to record their findings? Refer back to the learning outcomes on page 103.

Further work

If children need more practice in differentiating between fiction and non-fiction, provide the children with a selection of fiction and non-fiction books with dinosaurs as the subject/plot. Ask them to group them according to text type.

Provide a suitable non-fiction text on another animal and ask the children to find one main fact about where it lives, what it eats and what it looks like. Ask them to write the facts as brief notes.

DAY 1 ■ Watching an information programme

Key features	Stages	Additional opportunities
	Introduction Discuss the information the children found about dinosaurs and focus on the fact that they no longer exist. Explain the term *extinct* if necessary. Ask the children what they know about extinct animals, and discuss animals that are in danger of becoming extinct. Tell the class that they are going to watch a film or television programme about an animal in danger of extinction. Invite the children to suggest how information in a film or television documentary might differ from a book on the same topic. Explain that while they are watching the programme (copyright and ERA licence permitting), you will be making notes about the key points. Watch the programme.	
Communication: discuss the content and presentation of reports they are listening to	**Speaking and listening** Ask the children to describe what the programme was about to their response partners. Read the notes aloud that you made during the programme and discuss how you chose which points to record. Talk about and compare your notes with the children's oral summaries. **Independent work** Encourage the children write a summary of the programme in one sentence. **Plenary** Discuss what the children learned from the programme. Remind them of the differences they predicted and discuss the ways the information was presented, for example spoken words and moving images.	

DAY 2 ■ How oral information is presented

Key features	Stages	Additional opportunities
Enquiry: ask questions arising from work in another area of the curriculum **Information processing:** identify relevant information from a range of sources	**Introduction** Explain that the class will be watching another information programme about wildlife and exploring the different ways the information is presented. Watch the video from the CD-ROM 'Endangered species: Polar Bears'. Together compare the features of this video with the programme from yesterday. Discuss how the programmes use any of the following features: a visible presenter who speaks directly to the viewer, moving images with sound, a voice-over commentary where the speaker is not visible, when and how the information moves between different sections of information, how the programme is concluded. If available, watch other similar programmes and compare the styles of these as well. **Speaking and listening** Ask the children to work in groups and discuss how the information in the videos would be differently presented in a written text.	**ICT:** record wildlife documentaries broadcast on television or download from suitable websites, such as the discovery channel, bbc, or wwf.org.uk Allow time for the children to watch and listen (copyright and ERA licence permitting)
Social skills: listen to and respect others' viewpoints	**Independent work** Watch the programmes again and ask the children to make notes about the subject(s), for example the animal (or one of the animals) that is the subject, and its appearance, movement, feeding, where it lives and so on. **Plenary** Share and compare some of the children's notes.	

DAY 3 ■ An oral presentation

Key features	Stages	Additional opportunities
	Introduction Explain that the children will be working in small groups to plan and make a short presentation about the information they collected in their notes during the previous session. Review the features of the wildlife films they have watched, and discuss which features the children could use in their own presentations. Discuss whether they need to include visual information, sound effects and so on. Arrange the class into groups of three and ask them to collaborate in planning their presentations.	
Social skills: take on different roles within a group to complete a task	**Speaking and listening** Encourage the children to discuss which information they collected should be used in their presentations. Ask them to make decisions about the roles of each member. They should organise the information into the correct order and make brief notes as prompts. Tell them to draw or collect any visual information they want to include. Give the children time and the necessary resources to create their presentations.	**Support:** work with groups who need help to allocate roles for each member
Communication: present outcomes orally	**Plenary** Allow sufficient time for half of the groups to make their oral presentations to the class. Discuss and compare how groups had used the features they observed in the programmes, for example clear audible language, smooth transitions between points made and a clear conclusion.	

DAY 4 ■ Success criteria

Key features	Stages	Additional opportunities
Evaluation: discuss success criteria	**Introduction** Review the work done so far in this Unit. Ask the children to suggest how the information they read in the reports in Phase 1, and saw and heard in Phase 2 is similar and different.	
	Speaking and listening Explain that the class will be writing their own non-chronological reports in the next Phase of the Unit. Discuss the strategies they will need to use to create effective reports, for example researching information, note making, planning and writing, and write their suggestions on the board. Remind them about the typical language features and organisation of reports and add these to the board. Use the children's suggestions to agree points to use as success criteria for their individual report writing and draw up a list.	
Communication: present outcomes orally	**Plenary** Allow time for the remaining groups to make their oral presentations from the previous session. Discuss and compare how groups had used the features they observed in the programmes, for example clear audible language, smooth transitions between points made and a clear conclusion.	

Guided writing

Work with groups of children on note-making techniques, using abbreviations, key words, phrases and incomplete sentences to record the main points of a broadcast.

Assessment

Teacher observation and peer feedback: Do the children retain concentration while observing a presentation?
Are they able to use clear audible voices and link points in a logical way?
Is the information they included relevant to the topic?
Refer back to the learning outcomes on page 103.

Further work

Ask groups to make their oral presentations for children in a different class or during an assembly.

DAY 1 ■ Finding information

Key features	Stages	Additional opportunities
Information processing: identify relevant information from a range of sources	**Introduction** If possible, have a selection of books on the topics of birds and dinosaurs available. Explain that the class will be looking at the structure, language and features that are typical of non-chronological reports. Using one of the books as a model, Identify the title, and read the back cover blurb. Discuss with the class the importance of this information (it enables them to select the right book for their purposes). Ask the children to suggest how they would find specific information in the book. Find and read the contents page and the index. Model how to find a key word in the index using alphabetic knowledge and find the correct page. Point out any headwords and subheadings used to organise the text, and photographs or diagrams with captions and labels.	**Support:** display an enlarged copy of photocopiable page 118 'Reports'
	Speaking and listening Ask pairs of children to choose a book between them. Tell them to read the title and back cover, then to each write two questions they think the book might answer. Challenge them to swap their questions with their partner and try to look up the answers in the shortest time.	**Support:** write one question only, or do the activity orally
Communication: communicate outcomes orally	**Plenary** Encourage some of the children to tell the class what their questions were and describe the strategies they used to locate the answer, showing what they did with the book. Encourage them to use time-based connectives to structure their talk, such as *first* and *next*.	

DAY 2 ■ Paragraphs

Key features	Stages	Additional opportunities
Information processing: identify relevant information from a range of sources	**Introduction** Display the text *Birdwatcher's guide* from the CD-ROM. Read the extract to the class and ask them to say what sort of book this extract is from. Identify the headword *Tawny owl*. Point out and explain any difficult or unusual vocabulary, such as *Appearance, plumage, habitat*. Annotate the text, asking the children to identify different paragraphs. Identify the use of complete sentences in the information under the subheading *Appearance*. Ask the children to read the remaining paragraphs and say how the sentences differ, for example incomplete sentences and brief straight-to-the-point details. Discuss the punctuation with the children, ask: *Why don't statements such as* Woodland and trees *need a full stop?* Ask them to suggest other books they have read that use the same structure (encyclopedias, A-Z of...). Display an enlarged copy of photocopiable page 119 'Robin' and explain that you are going to rewrite some of the information as a paragraph. Model how to structure the sentences, orally rehearsing them, adding subjects and verbs and combining information.	
Communication: communicate outcomes orally and in writing	**Independent work** Provide the children with copies of the photocopiable sheet. Ask them to read the text and rewrite it into a single paragraph.	**Support:** use the first three paragraphs only
	Plenary Invite the children to read their paragraphs aloud. Discuss which structure they think makes the information quicker and easler to access.	

DAY 3 ▪ Explore a text

Key features	Stages	Additional opportunities
Information processing: identify relevant information from a range of sources	**Introduction** Display the extract *Birds* from the CD-ROM. Read the text to the class and ask them to suggest how this text differs from the one read in the previous session. Highlight any terms or information that is similar to the content of the previous text, for example *eggs, habitat, food*. Ask the children to identify the paragraphs and discuss why new paragraphs have been used, such as a change of subject. Encourage the children to find the verbs in the text. Discuss the reasons for the use of present tense (the text describes things that 'are' rather than 'were' or 'will be'). Ask the children to say what the subject of the text is (birds in general). Point out where the text gives specific examples to support a piece of information (*ostrich*). Invite some of the children to highlight other specific examples in the text. Let the children suggest what the purpose of the illustrations is.	
Social skills: listen to and respect others' viewpoints	**Independent work** Encourage the children to work with a partner and provide them with printed copies of the text. Ask them to discuss the illustrations and how the information could be enhanced by using labels and/or captions. Tell them to write a label or a caption for each of the illustrations.	**Support:** write labels only
	Plenary Ask the pairs of children to swap their copy with another pair. Invite them to give feedback about the labels and captions. Do they help readers understand the information in the text better?	

Guided reading

Select another report on the same or similar topic. Ask the children to read the contents page and index. Provide the children with specific questions to research. Ask them to use specific strategies to find the information, for example use the contents page, the index, scan the text. Support the children in reading the information.

Assessment

Peer assessment: Children give oral feedback.
Observation: Check that children can find key words in the index and use them to go to the correct page in the text. Check that they recognise the layout features of headings, subheadings, paragraphs, labels and captions.
Refer back to the learning outcomes on page 103.

Further work

Provide the children with other reports that have an index and ask them to locate specific information by using key words.
Ask children to find information in alphabetically-organised texts.

DAY 1 ◼ Planning the report

Key features	Stages	Additional opportunities
Enquiry: ask questions; plan how to present information effectively	**Introduction** Explain that the children are going to be writing their own reports about animals. Tell them that you will be going through the process with them on the board first by writing a report about 'animals in my neighbourhood', then they will be finding out information and making notes before writing their report for a class collection about animals. Display the Non-chronological report skeleton from the CD-ROM. Discuss with the class what sort of information the report should include, for example which animals are the subject of the report, are any in danger of extinction, what the animals look like, where they live, what they eat. Write their suggestions as headings on the skeleton. **Speaking and listening** Ask the children to work in groups and create a list of animals in their own neighbourhood. Write the children's suggestions on the skeleton. Then continue to add notes to the organiser, collaborating with the children about habitat (woods, underground, houses, trees, drains), food, appearance and so on, extending the skeleton to allow extra areas for adding detail on specific animals. **Plenary** Discuss with the children their lists of animals in the neighbourhood. Ask them to describe any facts about them they know. Discuss how they could find out more information to include in the report. Keep a copy of the skeleton plan for use in the later sessions.	

DAY 2 ◼ Model report

Key features	Stages	Additional opportunities
	Introduction Display the skeleton from the previous session. Discuss how you are going to organise the information. Explain that you want your report to have a short introduction, three main paragraphs and a short closing paragraph. Say that you need to focus on three different topics and suggest that you will use animals' habitats to organise the information. Amend, delete and rewrite your skeleton plan as needed to fit this structure, and show the three chosen topics for the three paragraphs, such as houses, streets and trees. Using the blank half of the Non-chronological skeleton from the CD-ROM, model writing your introduction, for example: *There are many different kinds of animals in our neighbourhood. They live in our houses, on the streets and even in the trees.* Demonstrate how to use capital letters and full stops. Point out the use of the comma in the second sentence. Draw the children's attention to the nouns, pointing out general terms about animals rather than specific vocabulary.	
Social skills: listen to and respect others' viewpoints	**Speaking and listening** Ask the groups of children to brainstorm different, more interesting headings to use for each paragraph. They could use single words or phrases.	**Support:** provide a thesaurus to help children
Communication: communicate outcomes orally	**Plenary** Take feedback about the groups' suggestions for paragraph headings. Choose the most appropriate ones and add them to the skeleton, for example *domestic animals, urban animals, tree livers* or similar. Keep a copy.	

DAY 3 ■ Writing demonstration

Key features	Stages	Additional opportunities
	Introduction Display the skeleton and notes from the previous session. Explain that you are going to demonstrate how to write some sentences for each of the three paragraphs. Write the opening sentences for the first paragraph, such as: *Domestic animals: Many people have animals as pets. These are usually cats, dogs or birds, such as parrots or budgies. These animals are fed using pet food which can be bought in shops. Some people keep reptiles, for example, snakes. Other people keep...* Encourage the children to suggest sentences that could be used for the next two paragraphs. Do not add them to the text at this point.	
Social skills: listen to and respect others' viewpoints	**Independent work** Ask the children to work with a partner and compose three sentences for each of the next two paragraphs. Tell them to discuss which information they think they should use before writing their sentences independently.	**Support:** work with children to support them if necessary
Communication: communicate outcomes orally and in writing	**Plenary** Return to the text and discuss the writing so far. Read it aloud and discuss the sentence structures. How do they sound? Ask the children to read some of their sentences from independent work and add them to the frame. Discuss, alter and explain spelling, grammar and punctuation as you write. Keep a copy for future use.	

DAY 4 ■ Writing a draft report

Key features	Stages	Additional opportunities
	Introduction Display the skeleton and notes on the board. Discuss how to write a concluding sentence or paragraph with the children. Take suggestions and model how to bring your report to a conclusion. Read the completed frame aloud. Explain that this is still only a draft of your report and it would need to be written without using the frame to be included in the class collection. Say that the children are going to write their own reports on this subject using the processes that you have been demonstrating. Display the skeleton notes from the first session. Explain that you want them to refer to the skeleton notes for ideas, but to write their draft reports using a copy of photocopiable page 120 'Report writing frame'.	
Enquiry: plan how to present information effectively	**Speaking and listening** Tell the children to work with a partner and talk about what they should include in their reports and how they should organise their ideas.	
	Independent work Ask the children to work independently to write their ideas in draft form using the writing frame.	**Support:** let children collaborate to write one report with their partner
Communication: communicate outcomes orally and in writing	**Plenary** Ask some of the children to read their draft reports aloud to the class. Discuss and compare the structure and layout. Did they all follow the layout that you modelled in the whole-class session? How do they differ?	

DAY 5 ■ Planning an encyclopedia

Key features	Stages	Additional opportunities
Information processing: identify relevant information from a range of sources and use this to write their own non-chronological reports	**Introduction** Explain that the children are going to write their own individual reports about animals for a class encyclopedia 'All About Animals'. Discuss the audience with the children: should it be for younger children or older ones? Discuss suitable subjects, for example: elephants, big cats, badgers, horses, whales, animals in danger. Provide copies of non-fiction books about the chosen subjects or allow children to select suitable texts from the library. Discuss other methods of researching information to use, such as the internet, television and film and magazines. **Speaking and listening** Allow time for the children to research information with a partner. Explain that they should make a decision about the topic, find out information on three key areas, such as where they live, what they look like, and what they eat. Ask them to also find out an unusual or surprising fact to include. Tell them to share their findings with each other and make notes on a non-chronological report skeleton. **Plenary** Invite some of the pairs of children to share their findings with the class. Discuss which were the most successful methods they found to research the information. Encourage some of the children to show their skeleton plans to the class. Ask them to say how helpful they found them in organising their research.	**ICT:** research information on the internet using websites such as www.discoverybroadband.co.uk/ or www.wwf.org.uk/gowild

DAY 6 ■ Writing frame

Key features	Stages	Additional opportunities
Enquiry: plan how to present information effectively	**Introduction** Display the skeleton and notes saved from Day 3 on the board. Explain that the children are going to use a copy of the writing frame to organise and draft their reports. Tell them they should refer to the notes they made on the skeleton organiser as a stimulus. Remind them about the audience for their reports and the purpose of an alphabetically-organised text. Ask them to suggest what important element is missing from the report on the board that is needed for an encyclopedia (headword). This will be needed when their reports are collected and put in the correct order. Remind the children to think about subheadings for their three paragraphs. Ask them to suggest suitable words or phrases that will signpost the information quickly and easily for younger readers.	
Evaluation: give feedback to others and judge the effectiveness of their own work	**Independent work** Provide a blank copy of photocopiable page 120 'Report writing frame' for each child. Ask them to write their ideas for a paragraph in each section. Ask them to work with a partner and discuss ideas for subheadings before adding or altering these to their drafts. Encourage the partners to read each other's drafts to check for meaning. Is the information about the animal clear? Tell them to check the grammar, spelling and punctuation. **Plenary** Ask some of the children to describe each other's reports and to say two things about it that deserve praise.	**Support:** write only one sentence in each section

DAY 7 ◼ Completing the encyclopedia

Key features	Stages	Additional opportunities
	### Introduction Explain to the children that they are going to complete their reports and they will be collected as an encyclopedia for the library. Discuss any additional non-fiction features that might enhance the information. Do they need any illustrations or diagrams? If so, should they add labels or captions? Ask the children to recall the research they did for their reports. Did any of them find an unusual or particularly interesting fact? Ask them to describe this information and discuss how to include it in their finished reports. Should it be included in one of the paragraphs, or made to stand out? Use shared writing to experiment with ways of highlighting the unusual fact in the report, such as a captioned fact box, 'Did you know?' or similar. Take suggestions from the class and agree on a common method.	
Evaluation: present information orally and in writing; discuss success criteria, give feedback and judge the effectiveness of their own work	### Independent work Ask the children to rewrite their drafts as polished reports, with a clear headword, introduction, three paragraphs with subheadings, and a conclusion. Tell them to add an illustration and label or caption and the fact box. ### Plenary Collect the children's work and, together, arrange it in the correct order to make an encyclopedia. Read the encyclopedia to the children. Review the children's objectives and success criteria for this Unit of work. Ask them to comment on what they have achieved and what needs further work.	**ICT:** use ICT to write polished reports

Guided writing

Support groups of children to write their reports during guided writing. Encourage them to use the features discussed in shared reading sessions, such as generalised vocabulary leading to specific examples, present tense and third person verbs. Encourage the group to swap and read each other's writing to check for meaning.

Assessment

Observation: Have the children used their research as a basis for their writing? Do they understand the benefit of planning their reports before writing the finished version? Does the completed encyclopedia follow a consistent style and layout?
Self assessment: Children evaluate their own work against the agreed success criteria.
Children can complete the CD-ROM assessment task 'Non-chronological reports'.
Refer back to the learning outcomes on page 103.

Further work

Ask the children to write further pages to add to the encyclopedia on different animals.

KWL Chart: Dinosaurs

What I KNOW about dinosaurs	What I WANT to know about dinosaurs	What I have LEARNED about dinosaurs

Reports

Tells us about a general class or group of things

Where they live or are found

What they look like

What they do

What they are used for

Layout

Contents page

Index

Headings

Subheadings

Paragraphs

Photographs

Diagrams

Captions

Labels

Language features

Present tense verbs

Third person verbs

Technical terms

Specific examples

Connectives to compare and contrast

Reports describe how things *are*

  100 LITERACY FRAMEWORK LESSONS YEAR 3   **PHOTOCOPIABLE**   **SCHOLASTIC**
www.scholastic.co.uk

Robin

■ Rewrite the information about robins as one paragraph at the bottom of the page.

Appearance	The robin is one of the more common, small birds in Britain. Their feathers are brown on their back and wings, with a red breast.
Habitat	All over; cities and woodlands
Nest	Well-made, from grass, roots, hair or wool. In many places, trees, shrubs or ledges.
Eggs	Five to eight, off-white and slightly speckled
Food	Insects and berries
Sounds	A varied song

_____

_____

_____

_____

_____

_____

_____

_____

_____

_____

_____

_____

_____

Report writing frame

Title:

Introduction:

Subheading:

Subheading:

Subheading:

Conclusion:

NON-FICTION
UNIT 2 Instructions

Speak and listen for a range of purposes on paper and on screen

Strand 1 Speaking
- Explain process and present information, ensuring that items are clearly sequenced, relevant details are included and accounts are ended effectively.

Strand 3 Group discussion and interaction
- Use discussion to organise roles and actions.
- Actively include and respond to all members of the group.

Read for a range of purposes on paper and on screen

Strand 6 Word structure and spelling
- Spell unfamiliar words using known conventions including grapheme/phoneme correspondences and morphological rules.

Strand 7 Understanding and interpreting texts
- Identify how different texts are organised, including reference texts, magazines and leaflets, on paper and on screen.

Write for a range of purposes on paper and on screen

Strand 9 Creating and shaping texts
- Make decisions about form and purpose, identify success criteria and use them to evaluate their writing.
- Select and use a range of technical and descriptive vocabulary.
- Use layout, format, graphics and illustrations for different purposes.

Strand 10 Text structure and organisation
- Signal sequence, place and time to give coherence.
- Group related material into paragraphs.

Strand 11 Sentence structure and punctuation
- Show relationships of time, reason and cause, through subordination and connectives.
- Compose sentences using adjectives, verbs and nouns for precision, clarity and impact.

Strand 12 Presentation
- Write with consistency in the size and proportion of letters and spacing within and between words, using the correct formation of handwriting joins.
- Develop accuracy and speed when using keyboard skills to type, edit and re-draft.

Progression in instructional texts

In this year children are moving towards:
- Reading and following instructions.
- Giving clear oral instructions to members of a group.
- Reading and comparing examples of instructional text, evaluating their effectiveness. Analysing more complicated instructions and identifying organisational devices which make them easier to follow.
- Researching a particular area and working in small groups to prepare a set of oral instructions. Trying out with other children, giving instruction and listening and following theirs. Evaluating effectiveness of instructions.
- Writing clear written instructions using correct register and devices to aid the reader.

UNIT 2 ◀ Instructions *continued*

Key aspects of learning covered in this Unit

Information processing
Children will process information from a range of media and use the information for their own instructional sequences.

Reasoning
Children will explain their opinion about the effectiveness of instructional texts against agreed criteria.

Evaluation
Children will have regular opportunities to watch videos of their own oral rehearsals and use these to improve their sequencing and use of imperative vocabulary.

Social skills
When orally rehearsing instructions children will learn about relating to the group members effectively.

Communication
Children will work collaboratively in paired, group and whole-class contexts. They will communicate outcomes orally, in writing and through ICT if appropriate.

Prior learning

Before starting this Unit check that the children can:
■ Respond to and follow both oral and written sequences of instructions.
■ Explain organisational features of texts, including alphabetical order, layout, diagrams, captions, hyperlinks and bullet points.
■ Compose sentences using present tense consistently (present, past and imperative).
If they need further support please refer to a prior Unit or a similar Unit in Year 2.

Resources

Phase 1:
How to make cheese on toast by Gillian Howell ✿; *Cheese on toast* by Gillian Howell ✿; Photocopiable page 134 'Clean teeth' ✿; Photocopiable page 135 'Features of instruction texts'; Videos or clips from children's 'how to...' television programmes; Instruction texts – from books, magazines or the internet

Phase 2:
Photocopiable page 136 'Instructions writing frame'; Digital video camera; Playback facilities; Cardboard boxes

Phase 3:
Photocopiable page 136 'Instructions writing frame'; Instructions skeleton ✿; Recipe ingredients and equipment; Assessment activity 'Sand castles'

Cross-curricular opportunities

Design and technology
Science

UNIT 2 ■ Teaching sequence

Phase	Children's objectives	Summary of activities	Learning outcomes
1	I can watch and discuss.	Watch an instructional programme and discuss language features. Paired talk giving instructions.	Children can recognise the structure and language features of an instructional text.
	I can identify features.	Analyse a shared text as a class and with a partner.	
	I can make notes.	Shared writing of instruction text. Make notes of a sequence of oral instructions.	Children can express a view clearly as part of a class or group discussion.
	I can compare texts.	Shared writing to improve instructions. Independently write a sentence.	
	I can contribute to success criteria.	Group discussion to agree whole-class success criteria.	
2	I can plan oral instructions.	Deconstruct a container and plan instructions for re-making it. Write a list of materials.	Children can orally produce instructions, evaluate their effectiveness and develop them into a chronological sequence.
	I can rehearse oral instructions.	Improve instructions. Videoed rehearsals of oral instructions.	
	I can write a draft.	Model writing of a set of instructions. Write a first draft of instructions.	
	I can refine drafts.	Rehearse and refine their instructions using videos. Research props and diagrams.	
	I can complete drafts.	Groups swap and compare instructions. Improve instructions from group feedback. Rehearse completed instructions.	
	I can present instructions.	Make and watch presentations.	
3	I can brainstorm ideas for healthy meals.	Model writing instructions for a recipe. Brainstorm recipes and agree on one for a class recipe.	Children can write an instructional text using selective adverbial language, sequenced imperative statements and presentational features such as bullet points or numbering.
	I can plan a recipe.	Use a skeleton and make notes.	
	I can polish notes.	Polish the draft to complete a set of instructions.	
	I can evaluate instructions.	Swap instructions in pairs and follow them.	

Provide copies of the objectives for the children.

DAY 1 ■ Watching instructions

Key features	Stages	Additional opportunities
Information processing: process information from a range of media	**Introduction** Explain to the children that they are going to be looking at the features and purposes of different instructional texts leading to writing their own. Brainstorm what the children already know about written instructions and their purposes, and draw up a list from their suggestions. Ask the children if they have read or watched any instructions recently. Discuss television programmes the children watch that feature instructions, such as art programmes, cookery programmes and so on. Ask them to suggest how an instructional television programme is similar to and different from written instructions. Record or download an extract from one of these programmes (copyright and ERA licence permitting) and play it for the class. Stop the programme at appropriate stages in order to discuss the order and sequence of steps being taken. Discuss the language features of oral instructions, and ask the children to repeat some of the verbs. Explain that these verbs are commands (imperative tense) and usually come at the beginning of a statement. Give the children some examples from everyday use, such as *come in*.	**ICT:** online sources for instructions include www.bbc.co.uk/cbbc/ and www.citv.co.uk
Communication: work collaboratively in paired contexts	**Speaking and listening** Ask the children to work in pairs and give each other instructions on how to get dressed for school.	
	Plenary Encourage the children to describe their oral instructions. How did they tell each other the order of steps? Did they use any connectives to show the sequence?	

DAY 2 ■ Common features

Key features	Stages	Additional opportunities
Information processing: process information from a range of sources	**Introduction** Display *How to make cheese on toast* from the CD-ROM. Read the text with the children and ask them to say what type of text this is. Identify the features, such as a clear title tells readers its purpose and what is needed is listed at the beginning, followed by a numbered sequence of steps. Annotate or highlight the features as you explain them. Ask the children to identify the verbs and circle them. Point out any statements which do not begin with an imperative verb, and identify connectives that signal time, or adverbs giving advice, such as *carefully*. Ask the children to identify any adjectives in the text. Point out that non-fiction texts use precise vocabulary, such as *white bread*, not *snow white bread*. Encourage the children to imagine they have never seen cheese on toast before. Discuss whether this set of instructions tells them everything they need to know.	**Support:** use *Cheese on toast* from the CD-ROM
Communication: communicate outcomes orally and in writing	**Speaking and listening** Provide the groups of children with a selection of simple instruction texts in books, magazines or from the internet. Ask them to read the instructions with a partner and note which features they all have in common.	**ICT:** printed instructions can be downloaded from the websites used in the previous session
	Plenary Discuss the children's findings and, together, draw up a list of the common features used in writing instructions.	

DAY 3 ■ Modelled writing

Key features	Stages	Additional opportunities
	Introduction Explain that you are going to demonstrate how to write a set of instructions about how to clean your teeth. Invite the children to describe what they did when they cleaned their teeth. Discuss the type of language they used in their descriptions. Ask them if their descriptions were instructions. Explain that their descriptions were recounts of what they did, using past tense verbs, but did not tell someone else how to do it using imperative verbs. Discuss whether any elements of their descriptions could be used to write the instructions, such as the sequence of steps. Model how to write the instructions, asking the children for suggestions about vocabulary choices. Keep a copy of the instructions.	
Social skills: relate to their partner when orally rehearsing instructions	**Speaking and listening** Ask the children to work with their partner from Day 1 and retell their oral sets of instructions for getting dressed. Tell them to make notes of the key statements and sequence. Ask the children if any of their oral instructions have changed since they first told them to their partner. Discuss why and how any changes have been made.	
	Independent work Provide children with copies of photocopiable page 134 'Clean teeth', having cut it into sections. Ask the children to sequence the sections into the correct order.	**Support:** read and sequence the photocopiable sheet with a partner
	Plenary Display the complete photocopiable sheet. Ask the children to compare their re-ordered set of instructions with the one on the board. Discuss any differences.	

DAY 4 ■ Effective or difficult?

Key features	Stages	Additional opportunities
	Introduction Remind the children of the instructions for cleaning teeth they looked at yesterday. Display photocopiable page 134 'Clean teeth' and ask the children to imagine they are aliens who have never needed to clean their teeth, and come from a planet without taps, water or toothpaste. Discuss what would be needed to make the instructions foolproof, for example extra detail, steps to the sequence and diagrams. Add to the instructions from the children's suggestions.	
Reasoning: explain their opinion about the effectiveness of instructional texts against agreed criteria	**Speaking and listening** Provide the children with the selection of simple instruction texts in books, magazines or from the internet that they used in Day 2. Ask them to read the instructions with a partner and think carefully about the list of equipment and the sequence of steps. Encourage them to discuss the instructions and decide which are the easiest to follow and why others are more difficult.	
	Independent work Let the children choose one set of easy-to-follow and one set of difficult instructions. Ask them to write a sentence to explain the difference between them.	**Support:** children compose the sentence orally with a partner
	Plenary Discuss the children's findings and ask some of them to describe a key fact that made the instructions effective.	

DAY 5 ▪ Success criteria: instructions

Key features	Stages	Additional opportunities
Reasoning: explain their opinion about the effectiveness of instructional texts	**Introduction** Display the completed set of instructions for cleaning teeth from shared writing on the board. Ask the children to discuss how effective they are, based on their analysis of effective instructions in the previous session. Explain to the class that they are going to collaborate in writing a list of the key features of effective written instructional texts and use this as part of a list of success criteria for their own writing.	**Support:** use photocopiable page 135 'Features of instruction texts' to help them identify the features
Communication: work collaboratively in group contexts	**Speaking and listening** Tell the children to work in groups and discuss which features they think are essential to effective instructions. Ask the group to nominate a secretary for the group to make notes and to report their ideas to the class.	
	Plenary Gather the groups together and take feedback from each group. Write their suggestions on the board, discuss them and amend until there is an agreed list of criteria. Ask the children to suggest other areas to include in the list, for example, spelling, grammar and punctuation.	

Guided reading
Provide the children with sets of instructions at an appropriate level. Ask children to identify language features, verbs, adverbs and adjectives.

Assessment
Observation: Do children recognise the structure and language features of instructional texts?
Are children able to distinguish between effective and difficult-to-follow instructions?
Do the children take part in group discussions and make contributions?
Refer back to the learning outcomes on page 123.

Further work
Ask children to work in different groups to read and analyse instructional texts. Let children annotate instructions to identify the key features.

DAY 1 ■ Plan an oral set of instructions

Key features	Stages	Additional opportunities
Communication: work collaboratively in whole-class contexts	**Introduction** Bring a selection of cardboard containers into the classroom before the session. Explain that the children are going to plan a set of instruction for making a box to keep a cake or sandwich in. Remind the children about the programmes they watched at the beginning of Phase 1 of the Unit. Explain that they are going to plan an oral presentation of the instructions in a similar style to a television programme. Brainstorm ideas for making a box and write the children's suggestions on the board. Ask the children to describe the essential features of their instructions. Will these be different from the features of written instructions? *← make different item*	
Communication: work collaboratively in whole-class contexts	**Speaking and listening** Ask the children to deconstruct one of the boxes in small groups and work out what it is made from. Ask them to discuss how to make a similar box. Tell them to make notes as they talk to list resources needed. Tell them to orally rehearse the sequence of steps needed to make the box. Allow time to try out different orders of steps in the sequence orally.	**Support:** work with groups to support them in sequencing the steps
	Independent work Ask the children to write a list of materials needed.	
	Plenary Discuss the project with the class. Explain that you will be using a digital video camera to record their rehearsals to allow them to alter and improve the presentations.	

DAY 2 ■ Rehearsing and recording

Key features	Stages	Additional opportunities
	Introduction Explain that the children are going to work in their groups to improve the detail of the instructions needed for their presentations. Ask them to feed back what each group did in the previous session and discuss what they need to do to improve their instructions. *CITV STYLE SHOW*	
Communication: work collaboratively in group contexts	**Speaking and listening** Ask the children to collaborate in their groups to go through the sequence of their instructions orally. Encourage them to nominate a secretary to keep notes of their progress. Ask the groups to rehearse a presentation of the instructions. Record each group using the digital video camera. Remember to obtain parents' or carers' permission before recording the children. Allow time for the groups to watch their video recordings.	**Support:** arrange groups so that a more confident learner can act as secretary; use the instruction skeleton from the CD-ROM to help sequence the steps
Evaluation: watch videos of oral rehearsals and use these to improve their sequencing	**Plenary** Ask the children to report on their group's progress. Discuss any difficulties the children are experiencing. Invite the children to suggest what else is needed to make their instructions clear in an oral presentation, for example *Would diagrams and illustrations help make the instructions clear?*	

DAY 3 ■ Draft instructions

Key features	Stages	Additional opportunities
	### Introduction
Explain that the children are going to begin to write their instructional sequence as a draft. Remind the children of the instructions written in the first Phase of this Unit and the key features. Ask one of the groups to describe their plans for making their box so far and model how to write them in draft form. Read them aloud and orally demonstrate your thoughts: *Is there a step missing here? Should I put step three before step two? Have I spelled that word correctly? Does this need to go in the list of materials and equipment?*	
Evaluation: watch videos of oral rehearsal and use these to improve sequencing	### Speaking and listening
Let some of the children to watch the videos of their rehearsals to identify areas that need further work.	
	### Independent work
Tell the children to revise the list of the resources needed from Day 1, and write a draft of the instruction sequence.
Ask half the group to use their drafts to rehearse orally, while the other half of the group observe and check that the sequence is logical and easy to follow, and that imperative verbs are used correctly.	**Support:** use photocopiable page 136 'Instructions writing frame' as a support
Communication: work collaboratively in group contexts	### Plenary
Discuss the children's progress with them. Invite them to suggest what they have learned from watching their first rehearsals of the instructions. Does it help them learn what they need to do?	

DAY 4 ■ Refining instructions

Key features	Stages	Additional opportunities
	### Introduction
Explain that the groups of children are going to rehearse and refine their instructions.	
Evaluation: watch videos of oral rehearsals and use these to improve their sequencing and use of imperative vocabulary	### Speaking and listening
Ask the groups to use their drafts and go through their presentations while you make another video of them.
Allow time for the groups to watch their new rehearsals and discuss how they have improved from the first versions. Discuss what props would help make them clearer for a viewer, such as diagrams and other graphics.	
Social skills: learn about relating to group members effectively	### Independent work
Ask the groups to allocate roles for researching and creating the necessary props using drawings and graphics. Tell them to rehearse the sequence once more using the diagrams and other graphics. Encourage them to revise their drafts to include these new elements.	**Support:** work with groups who need support to research graphics
	### Plenary
Review the children's progress. Remind them about the films of televised instructions they watched in Phase 1. Ask the children to suggest which aspects of these presentations they could incorporate in their own presentations of their instructions.	

DAY 5 ■ Final rehearsal

Key features	Stages	Additional opportunities
Evaluation: feed back opinions about others' work **Communication:** work collaboratively in group contexts	**Introduction** Tell the children they are going to swap their draft instruction sequences with another group, to read and see if they can follow them. **Speaking and listening** Encourage the groups to feed back their responses to each other's drafts. Are the instructions written in a clear sequence? Will they result in making a cake or sandwich box? Have all the materials and resources that are referred to in the sequence of steps been listed at the start of the draft? Are they listed in the order they will be used? **Independent work** Ask the groups to collect their own draft instructions and make any changes they need to, based on the group feedback. Tell the groups to allocate final roles for presenting their oral instruction to the class. Remind them of any presentational features they could use from the broadcast programmes they watched previously. Explain that the outcome of this part of their work on instructions is not a written but an oral outcome. Ask the groups to rehearse their completed draft instructions. **Plenary** Ask some of the children to describe what their presentations will contain, and what roles they will play.	**Support:** work with groups to analyse feedback and identify areas for improvement

DAY 6 ■ Class presentations

Key features	Stages	Additional opportunities
Social skills: learn about relating to the other group members effectively **Evaluation:** watch videos of their own rehearsals and use these to improve their sequencing and use of imperative vocabulary	**Introduction** Allow time for the children in their groups to rehearse their instruction sequence using the completed drafts. **Speaking and listening** Ask each group to present their instructions orally to the whole class. Make a final video of each presentation. Discuss each group's instructions with the class. Did they use clear, audible voices? Were the instructions easy to follow and in a logical sequence? Did each member of the group make a contribution? Were the materials clearly explained at the beginning? Did the children use imperative verbs and precise vocabulary? Discuss other audiences for their instructions. Make the videos available for other children to watch, or upload them onto the school website if you have obtained the relevant permission from parents or carers. **Plenary** Play the videos to the children. Ask the groups to comment on their own presentations of their instructions. Discuss the targets for the Unit and success criteria, and ask children to say what they have achieved and what needs further work.	**Extend:** follow the instructions to make a box

Guided writing

Work with groups writing their draft instructions. Discuss choices for imperative verbs and add new verbs to personal dictionaries.

Assessment

Self assessment: Children review their progress toward targets by evaluating their final instruction presentations. Refer back to the learning outcomes on page 123.

Further work

Ask children to use their drafts to write a polished set of instructions.
Use printed instructions from books as a stimulus for children to present orally.

DAY 1 ■ Writing instructions

Key features	Stages	Additional opportunities
Information processing: process information from a range of media and use the information for their own instructional sequences	### Introduction Review the work done so far in this Unit. Tell the children that they are going to be writing their own instruction texts to be collected for a class display. Discuss topics for the book with the children and encourage them to agree on a recipe for Healthy Food. Use the Instructions skeleton from the CD-ROM to model writing a recipe for a salad. Say how recipes use the term *ingredients* as a heading for 'what is needed'. Demonstrate your thought processes as you list the ingredients. Explain the need for precise use of quantities in order that the instructions lead to the correct outcome. Write the sequence of steps, orally checking that the order follows a logical sequence. Discuss the other headings used in a recipe. Explain that the sequence of steps is called *The Method*. Keep a copy of your work.	
Communication: work collaboratively in groups	### Speaking and listening Ask the children to work in groups and brainstorm a list of meals and snacks that could feature in a recipe book for Healthy Eating. Take feedback and write the list on the board. Agree on a single meal, such as tuna salad wrap. If possible choose a meal that is available as a school lunch. Discuss the ingredients for the meal and ask the children to suggest the method and sequence of making it. Keep a copy.	**Further reading:** provide copies of recipe books to stimulate ideas **Extend:** use the internet to research healthy food
	### Plenary Ask the children to suggest the process they will use to write a finished recipe.	

DAY 2 ■ Making notes on a skeleton

Key features	Stages	Additional opportunities
	### Introduction Display your modelled salad recipe on the board. Ask volunteers to identify the key features of instructions, one at a time. Point out examples where you have used adverbs, such as *carefully*. Ask the children to suggest reasons for using adverbs to qualify a step. Explain that the children are going to write their own recipes for a tuna salad wrap or whichever meal was agreed on in the previous session. Ask the children to say what they remember of the brainstorm session from yesterday. Discuss what is essential to include for a recipe outcome to be effective.	
Communication: work collaboratively in paired contexts	### Independent work Provide pairs of children with the instructions skeleton and ask them to collaborate with each other to make notes for planning their recipe. They should talk about what is needed, how many steps and their order, and write brief notes on the skeleton. Ask them to begin writing their recipes using photocopiable page 136 'Instructions writing frame'.	**Extend:** begin writing their recipes without using the writing frame
Communication: communicate outcomes orally	### Plenary Ask some of the children to share their skeleton plans with the class. Discuss and compare their lists of ingredients and sequence of steps. Let those who have begun writing a draft describe their progress. Ask them to describe what their next step will be to progress towards a polished written outcome.	

DAY 3 ▬ Writing a recipe

Key features	Stages	Additional opportunities
Reasoning: explain their opinion about the effectiveness of instructional texts against agreed criteria	**Introduction** Explain that the children are going to finish the drafts and then write them as polished recipes. **Speaking and listening** Ask pairs of children to discuss their skeletons and drafts and suggest improvements. **Independent work** Encourage the children to work independently to finish their drafts of instructions. Tell them to swap them with their response partners and make suggestions for improvement. Are all the ingredients listed, are the amounts and quantities correct, are the ingredients written in the right order, do the steps follow a logical sequence? Ask the children to respond to the feedback and make any improvements that are needed. Let them write their polished versions. **Plenary** Remind the children about the success criteria. Ask some of the children to share their finished recipes with the class. Discuss and compare their sequence of steps. How are they similar of different? Is there anything that could improve the instructions?	**ICT:** use a computer to write recipes

DAY 4 ▬ Following a recipe

Key features	Stages	Additional opportunities
	Introduction Ask the children to suggest what the best way to judge the effectiveness of a set of instructions might be. Elicit that following the instructions and reaching the correct outcome easily would show how effective they are. Explain that the children are going to work in pairs and follow the recipes of different children. Before commencing this activity, ensure to check for any food allergies or dietary requirements. **Independent work** Provide the ingredients and equipment needed to follow the children's recipes. Ask the children to read one of the recipes carefully, collect what is needed, and follow the steps in the sequence.	**Health:** explain about hygiene and safety when handling food
Reasoning: evaluate the effectiveness of instructional texts against agreed criteria	**Plenary** Ask the children to report on how easy or difficult they found it to follow the recipe and give reasons for their opinions. Is there anything that could improve them? Encourage the children to eat the outcome of the activity, providing they have no food allergies or dietary requirements.	

Guided writing

Work with children during guided writing to draft, edit and improve their recipe writing.

Assessment

Peer assessment: Feedback related to following instructions practically.
Teacher assessment: Have the children used appropriate adjectives, sequential steps and bullet points or numbered steps?
Children complete the assessment activity 'Sand castles' on the CD-ROM. Refer back to the learning outcomes on page 123.

Further work

Encourage the children to read and explore the features of other types of instructional texts, such as directions and safety instructions.
Children could write a set of instructions for hygiene while making food.

Clean teeth

■ Cut out the sections to re-order in the correct sequence of instructions.

✂

How to clean your teeth
What you need:
a tube of toothpaste a toothbrush water a towel
What you do:
Squeeze a small ball of toothpaste onto the toothbrush.
Wet the toothbrush.
Brush the toothpaste all over your teeth.
Keep brushing for 2 minutes.
Rinse the toothbrush.
Then rinse your mouth with the water.
Dry your mouth with the towel.

Features of instruction texts

Organisation and layout

Clear aim

List of what is needed

Clear sequence of steps

Numbers or bullet points

Diagrams

Language features

Specific details (number, size, temperature)

Imperative verbs at the beginning of sentences

Time connectives

Adverbs 'how'

Precise factual adjectives

Instructions tell you how to do something

NON-FICTION ■ UNIT 2

Instructions writing frame

List everything!	Aim:
	What is needed:
Sequence of steps **Command verbs** **Factual adjectives** **Time-connectives**	What to do: • • • • • • • • •
	Diagram(s) or illustration(s):

NON-FICTION
UNIT 3 Information texts

Speak and listen for a range of purposes on paper and on screen

Strand 1 Speaking
- Explain process or present information, ensuring items are clearly sequenced, relevant details are included and accounts ended effectively.

Strand 3 Group discussion and interaction
- Use discussion to organise roles and actions.
- Actively include and respond to all members of the group.

Read for a range of purposes on paper and on screen

Strand 7 Understanding and interpreting texts
- Identify how different texts are organised, including reference texts, magazines and leaflets, on paper and on screen.

Strand 8 Engaging with and responding to texts
- Identify features that writers use to provoke readers' reactions.

Write for a range of purposes on paper and on screen

Strand 9 Creating and shaping texts
- Make decisions about form and purpose, and identify success criteria for their writing.
- Write non-narrative texts using structures of different text-types.
- Select and use a range of descriptive and technical vocabulary.
- Use layout, format, graphics and illustrations for different purposes.

Strand 10 Text structure and organisation
- Signal sequence, place and time to give coherence.
- Group related material into paragraphs.

Strand 11 Sentence structure and punctuation
- Show relationships of time, reason and cause through subordination and connectives.
- Compose sentences using adjectives, verbs and nouns for precision, clarity and impact.

Strand 12 Presentation
- Develop accuracy and speed when using keyboard skills to type, edit and re-draft.

Progression in information texts

In this year children are moving towards:
- Recalling to mind, existing knowledge on a subject and reducing the options for enquiry by posing focused questions.
- Beginning to use library classification to find reference materials and scanning indexes, directories and IT sources to locate information quickly.
- Making clear notes by identifying key words, phrases or sentences in reading and making use of simple formats to capture key points.
- Beginning to use graphic organisers as a tool to support collection and organisation of information.
- Recounting the same event in a variety of ways.
- Deciding how to present information and making informed choices.
- Using computers to bring information texts to published form with appropriate layout, font and so on.

UNIT 3 ◄ **Information texts** *continued*

■ Creating multi-media information texts.

Key aspects of learning covered in this Unit

Enquiry
Children will ask questions, research and then plan how to present the information effectively.

Information processing
Children will identify relevant information from a range of sources on paper and on screen.

Evaluation
Children will present information orally and in writing. They will discuss success criteria, give feedback to others and judge the effectiveness of their own work.

Social skills
When developing collaborative writing, children will learn to listen to and respect others' viewpoints and take on different roles within a group to complete a task.

Communication
Children will work collaboratively in paired, group and whole-class contexts. They will communicate outcomes orally, in writing and through ICT, if appropriate.

Reasoning
Children will explain their opinion about the effectiveness of simple persuasive texts against agreed criteria.

Prior learning

Before starting this Unit check that the children can:
■ Write three facts about something that interests them in three sentences, using capital letters and full stops (and commas for lists, if appropriate), consistently using the present tense and precise vocabulary.
■ Explain organisational features of texts, including alphabetical order, layout, diagrams, captions, hyperlinks and bullet points.
If they need further support please refer to a prior Unit or a similar Unit in Year 2.

Resources

Phase 1:
Crossing the road from www.highwaycode.gov.uk ✥; *How to cross the road* by Gillian Howell ✥; *The Green Cross Code* from www.hedgehogs.gov.uk ✥; Photocopiable page 153 'KWL Chart'; Photocopiable page 154 'Questions'; Resources for research

Phase 2:
Air-filled cushions by Gillian Howell ✥; Photocopiable page 155 'Persuasion'; Photocopiable page 156 'Advertising'; Persuasion skeleton ✥; Simple persuasive texts – advertisements, leaflets, magazines, newspapers

Phase 3:
Digital camera

Phase 4:
Photocopiable page 118 'Reports'; Photocopiable page 135 'Features of instruction texts'; Report skeleton ✥; Instruction skeleton ✥; Recount skeleton ✥; Slideshow software; Assessment activity 'Labels' ✥; Around the town ✥

Cross-curricular opportunities

PSHE

UNIT 3 ■ Teaching sequence

Phase	Children's objectives	Summary of activities	Learning outcomes
1	I can contribute to class discussion.	Introduction of the topic road safety and class and group discussion.	Children can make informed choices for research based on their prior knowledge.
	I can explore a topic.	Group discussion to identify areas for research. Fill in KWL charts.	Children can note information collected from a range of sources.
	I can make decisions.	Model writing using a KWL chart. Write a list of questions.	
	I can find answers.	Discuss in groups, allocate research methods. Paired research.	
	I can recognise the features of instructions.	Shared reading, group discussion of text types. Continue paired research.	
	I can recognise the features of reports.	Modelled writing on changing text type. Continue and complete paired research.	
2	I can recognise the features of simple persuasive texts.	Shared reading of a persuasive text. Explore other texts in groups.	Children can recognise the features and purpose of simple persuasive texts.
	I can contribute to role play.	Class discussion on the features of advertisements. Partner role play.	Children can express a view clearly as part of a class or group discussion.
	I can create an advertisement.	Model writing of a poster. Paired writing to plan an advertisement.	
		Class discussion on visual effects. Polish their writing.	
3	I can plan a role play.	Whole-class discussion and group planning of a role-play presentation.	Children can use clear persuasive language in an oral presentation.
	I can choose dialogue.	Rehearse their role play in groups and focus on persuasive vocabulary.	
	I can perform a role play.	Group performances of role play. Write a paragraph to recount their individual role.	
4	I can plan a report.	Class discussion on planning a non-chronological report and group discussion. Use a report skeleton to create a plan.	Children can use notes collected from a range of sources and present them in different forms including ICT and evaluate their effectiveness.
	I can write a report.	Write paragraphs for group reports.	
	I can plan and write instructions.	Use previous research to plan and write instructions with partners.	
	I can plan a recount.	Class discussion on recounts. Independent writing using recount skeletons.	
	I can write a recount.	Brainstorm a list of temporal connectives. Independent writing of recounts.	
	I can plan a presentation.	Group discussion on planning an ICT presentation of work. Save work on a computer.	
	I can create an ICT presentation.	Create and view a slideshow presentation.	

Provide copies of the objectives for the children.

DAY 1 ■ Road safety

Key features	Stages	Additional opportunities
	Introduction Explain that the children will be exploring the subject of roads, traffic and road safety, and experimenting with different ways of presenting information about this theme. Ask the children to describe how they get to school each day. Focus on pavements and roads that any of the children use, and ask them to comment on how they keep themselves safe. Talk about crossing places, school crossing patrols, zebra crossings and so on. Brainstorm what the children already know about road safety and draw up notes on the board. Encourage the children to suggest how they would find out more information, for example books, leaflets, the internet or asking an adult. Ask them what sort of texts they should be looking for, such as non-fiction information texts.	
Communication: work collaboratively in group contexts	**Speaking and listening** Ask the children to work in groups and discuss areas for research on the themes of roads and road safety. Ask them to draw up a list.	**Support:** work with groups to stimulate ideas
	Plenary Gather the children together and take feedback from the groups. Create a list of the areas they suggest and add to it if needed. Aim to include some of the following aspects of the subject: cars, lorries, motorways, speed, accident prevention, the Green Cross Code, keeping safe. Explain that each group will be collecting information about a different area using a range of sources.	

DAY 2 ■ Finding information

Key features	Stages	Additional opportunities
	Introduction Say that the children are going to begin researching information for their group area of the subject. Allocate an area to each group. Remind the children about their suggestions of how and where to look for information and draw up a list for reference.	
Communication: working collaboratively in group contexts	**Speaking and listening** Ask the groups to discuss the strategies they will use to research information and to share the tasks between all members of the group, for example using the class library, the school library, the internet, asking an adult.	
Enquiry: ask questions	**Independent work** Provide each child with a copy of photocopiable page 153 'KWL Chart'. Ask the children to make notes of what they already know about the subject they will be researching, such as traffic speed, and what they want to know about it.	**Support:** work with a partner to share information and fill in the chart
Evaluation: discuss success criteria	**Plenary** Ask the groups to share the notes. Discuss the *What I WANT to know* column. Explain that, if they decide in advance what they want to find out, it will make their research more focused and easier to find information, for example, if they are going to 'ask an adult' as their research method, they will need to think of questions to ask in advance. Draw up a list of success criteria for research, such as deciding what they want to know, using a variety of sources, making notes of their findings.	

DAY 3 ■ Questions

Key features	Stages	Additional opportunities
Enquiry: ask questions	### Introduction Use modelled and shared writing with the class to demonstrate how to decide what information you want to find on an area of the subject, for example, demonstrate using 'traffic speed'. Display an enlarged copy of photocopiable page 153 'KWL Chart', and demonstrate your thought processes aloud for the class, for example: *I know that roads have different speed limits, but I don't know what they are, or how many different ones. So I need to find out.* Continue until you have three or four notes in the *What I WANT to know* column, such as: *Speed limits? What? How many?* Demonstrate how to write these points as questions, asking the children to tell you how they should be punctuated.	
	### Independent work Ask the children to return to their KWL charts, add any further points to the middle column and then to write them as full sentences with correct punctuation. Encourage the group to share their lists of questions with each other.	**Support:** revise the punctuation of questions using photocopiable page 154 'Questions'
Communication: communicate outcomes orally and in writing	### Plenary Ask the groups to read their lists of questions for each area for research. Discuss the different sorts of questions, for example: *Where would you find out this information? Do they think the answers will be facts or will they be someone's own point of view or opinion?*	

DAY 4 ■ Finding answers

Key features	Stages	Additional opportunities
	### Introduction Provide a range of resources for the children to use for research, for example non-fiction books, newspaper and magazine articles and access to ICT. Explain that, in this session, the children will begin to find out the answers to their lists of questions. Ask the children to suggest which adults they think could give them information, for example a teacher, the headteacher, the crossing-patrol person. Encourage them to suggest why they should choose a specific person. Discuss how to locate the appropriate area of the library.	
Social skills: take on different roles within a group **Communication:** work collaboratively in pairs	### Speaking and listening Ask the children to discuss in their groups which methods they will use to research the information. Tell them to discuss how to share the methods within the group, for example, whether they should focus on their own personal list or collect all the questions that will be researched using a single source, such as the internet or the library. Let the children then allocate different roles to pairs within the group.	**Support:** the teacher allocates methods of research to pairs **ICT:** suitable websites on road safety include www.hedgehogs.gov.uk www.thinkroadsafety.gov.uk www.bbc.co.uk
Information processing: identify relevant information from a range of sources	### Independent work Ask children to work with a partner to research answers to their list questions using a range of resources. Tell them to write them on their KWL chart for use later.	
	### Plenary Gather the children together and ask some of the groups to describe their research methods to the others, and how successful they were. Ask them to describe any obstacles they have encountered.	

DAY 5 ■ Different text types

Key features	Stages	Additional opportunities
Information processing: identify relevant information from a range of sources	### Introduction Explain to the children that they will be using the information from their research to make a slideshow presentation about the topic later in the Unit. Review the different types of text the children are familiar with and what their purposes are. Which text types would suit the information they are researching? Display *Crossing the road* and *The Green Cross Code* from the CD-ROM. Read the texts to the children and ask them to say what type of texts these are (instructions). Identify the features, similarities and differences in both texts. Ask the children: *Is anyone researching this information? Has anyone found information about school crossing patrols, toucan crossings, traffic wardens?* Invite the children to suggest how the information in these texts might be written using another text type. ### Speaking and listening Have a range of different types of text available and ask groups to look at a variety and discuss which type of text would suit the information they are researching, for example a report, a diary or an alphabetically-ordered text. ### Independent work Let the children continue researching the answers to questions on their KWL charts. ### Plenary Ask the children to suggest which type of text they would use for their presentation and why.	**MFW:** below, until, children, always, first, place, between, before, around, any, suddenly **Support:** use *How to cross the road* from the CD-ROM

DAY 6 ■ Changing text type

Key features	Stages	Additional opportunities
Information processing: identify relevant information from a range of sources **Evaluation:** discuss success criteria, give feedback and judge the effectiveness of their own work	### Introduction Explain to the class that you are going to show the children how to use some of the information from one type of text to write in a different text type. Display *Crossing the road* from the CD-ROM and explain that you want to write a non-chronological report about safe places to cross the road in your area. Model the process by underlining key words on the text, such as: *subway, footbridge, zebra, pelican, toucan, parked cars, brow of hills, school crossing patrol, police officer*. Use the Non-chronological report skeleton from the CD-ROM to model organising headings (such as *safe places, unsafe places, people who help*) and adding information around the headings. Model using one heading and the notes to write an opening sentence, a subheading and one short paragraph. Ask the children to suggest what changes would need to be made to rewrite the text as a recount (first or third person, past tense verbs). ### Independent work Ask children to continue and finish researching the answers to their list of questions with their partner, and complete the final column of their KWL charts. ### Plenary Review the success criteria for researching information with the children. Discuss how successful the children have been. Ask if there are any questions that remain unanswered and what the reason is. Discuss whether any of their questions were unanswerable. Keep the research for use in later Phases.	**Support:** display a summary chart of text-type features

Guided writing

Use guided writing to write questions in different structures, such as using question words: *who, what, where, why* and *how*; reversing subject and verb: *he is, is he*; using question marks.

Assessment

Observation: Have the children written answerable questions for their research? Do they use correct punctuation?

Peer assessment: Do the children collaborate with and contribute to their group?

Refer back to the learning outcomes on page 139.

Further work

Use photocopiable page 154 'Questions' to provide practice and consolidation on writing questions.

DAY 1 ■ Persuasion

Key features	Stages	Additional opportunities
	## Introduction Provide a selection of simple persuasive texts for the classroom, particularly advertisements (such as for new cars) and other leaflets, pamphlets and posters. Display the advertisement for *Air-filled cushions* from the CD-ROM. Mask or hide the last lines (*These special...* onwards). Read the text to the children and ask them to say what the purpose of it is. Is it giving them information? Is it an instruction? Reveal the hidden part of the text and read it to the children. Elicit the fact that this is an advertisement. Ask the children to say what they think the purpose of an advertisement is. Tell the children that an advertisement's purpose is to persuade the reader to buy or use something. Ask the children to describe other advertisements they have seen or watched on television. Go through the text and discuss the features, such as questions that they already know the answer to, words to make readers feel worried (*serious!!!*), lots of exclamation marks, print used to get your attention. Ask the children why they think the line regarding availability is in smaller print. Ask them if there are any features similar to instructions, such as *read, attach, hurry* (imperative verbs).	**MFW:** children, every, sometimes
Communication: work collaboratively in groups	## Speaking and listening Ask the children to work in groups and look at the persuasive texts you have provided. Challenge them to see if they can find any of the features you have discussed as a whole class.	**Support:** work with groups who need extra support to identify persuasive features
Evaluation: discuss success criteria	## Plenary Discuss their responses and agree criteria for effective persuasive texts.	

DAY 2 ■ Advertise it!

Key features	Stages	Additional opportunities
	## Introduction Ask the children to describe television advertisements they are familiar with. Discuss how effective they are: *Do they make you want to have the thing being advertised? Do they make you think you really need it? Why is this? How do they do it?* Remind the children about the advertisement they looked at in the previous session. Ask them to recall as many of the features that they remember. Draw up a list and add to it if necessary.	**Support:** display a copy of photocopiable page 155 'Persuasion'
Communication: work collaboratively in pairs	## Speaking and listening Explain to the children that you want them to work in pairs. Tell them to role play being in a television advertisement, one at a time, and to try and persuade their partner to buy something. You could choose the item to sell for the children, or they choose it themselves.	
Reasoning: explain their opinion about the effectiveness of simple persuasive texts **Social skills:** listen to and respect others' viewpoints	## Plenary Discuss the children's role playing with the class. Which children felt they wanted to have the item being advertised? Ask them to give a show of hands. Discuss with the others why the advertisement failed to persuade them. Ask some of the successful advertisers to perform their role play for the class, and then some of the unsuccessful advertisers. Discuss and compare their similarities and differences. Encourage the children to look out for persuasive features in television advertising when they are at home.	

DAY 3 ■ Plan an advertisement

Key features	Stages	Additional opportunities
	Introduction Ask the children to feed back about any advertisements they have watched on television since the last session. Discuss any persuasive features they recognised. *Did any of the advertisements ask a question? Did they make you want to have it? Why?* Ask the children to suggest how television advertising differs from advertising on paper, such as magazines and posters. Explain that you want them to write a poster to replace their role-play advertisement. Model how to do this on the Persuasion skeleton from the CD-ROM, rehearsing your points orally and thinking aloud. Experiment with different coloured pens, sizes of print and so on.	
Social skills: listen to and respect others' viewpoints	**Independent work** Ask the children to work with the same partner as yesterday, discuss ideas and to collaborate to design an advertisement between them in note form. Encourage them to experiment with colours, lettering and punctuation.	**Support:** use the prompts on photocopiable page 156 'Advertising' to help them organise their points
	Plenary Discuss the plans with the children. Ask some of them to describe the features they are using to make their advertisements persuasive. Remind them to tell the reader to buy it (give an instruction).	

DAY 4 ■ Polish the advertisement

Key features	Stages	Additional opportunities
	Introduction Display some of the advertisements and other persuasive posters and leaflets that you have provided. Look at them with the children and discuss which ones they think attract their attention most. Ask the children to give reasons (for example, eye-catching illustrations, bright colours, variations in print sizes or layouts). Discuss what the children could do to make their advertisements stand out.	
Social skills: listen to and respect others' ideas	**Speaking and listening** Tell the children to discuss their plans for the advertisement with their partners and to think of ideas to improve the visual effect.	
	Independent work Ask the children to write their advertisements and use drawings, pictures and other effects to enhance their work.	**Extend:** use ICT to create their advertisements and enhance them with clip art
Reasoning: explain their opinion about the effectiveness of simple persuasive texts against agreed criteria	**Plenary** Display the children's advertisements on a wall in the classroom. Review the success criteria for effective persuasive texts. Ask the children to say what they have done to achieve success and what they still need to do to progress. Discuss other reasons why persuasive texts might be written, for example safety advice.	

Guided reading

Read a persuasive text with the group and identify language features, such as imperative verbs, incomplete sentences, use of questions and punctuation.

Assessment

Observation: Can the children explain their responses to persuasive texts? Are they able to differentiate between questions, statements and instructions?

Refer back to the learning outcomes on page 139.

Further work

Provide advertisements from magazines and newspapers. Ask the children to mark the sentences according to question, statement, and instruction.

DAY 1 ■ Plan a role play

Key features	Stages	Additional opportunities
Communication: work collaboratively in group contexts and take on different roles	### Introduction Remind the children of the research they did in Phase 1 on the themes of roads and road safety. Explain that they are going to use their research in order to make a group presentation using a range of approaches including role play. Discuss the children's different topic areas and ask them to suggest how they could enact part of their findings in a persuasive way, for example crossing the road safely, not speeding, buying a new car. Write a list of the children's suggestions. ### Speaking and listening Ask the children to work in their groups and plan a role play using their research topics. They should allocate roles among all members of the group. Encourage them to practise and experiment with different versions, swapping roles within the group. ### Plenary Gather the children together and discuss the progress of their role-play plans. Discuss and compare the different scenes the groups have chosen, and ask some of the groups to describe what will happen in their role play.	**Support:** work with some groups to help them plan and allocate roles **Extend:** plan a role play to persuade other children to use the Green Cross Code

DAY 2 ■ Persuasive words

Key features	Stages	Additional opportunities
Social skills: take on different roles within a group to complete a task **Evaluation:** give feedback and judge the effectiveness of their own work	### Introduction Remind the children about the features of persuasive texts. Ask them to suggest how they can include some of these in their role-play scenes. For example, can they ask a question which has an obvious answer, such as *Do you* want *to get knocked over?* Encourage the children to suggest how they can include statements and instructions. How are they going to persuade someone to do something, or change the way they behave? ### Speaking and listening Ask the children to rehearse their role-play scenes in their groups. Encourage them to focus on what dialogue they will include, how to say it, and to ensure every member of the group makes a contribution. Give the children enough time to complete their scenes. ### Plenary Ask some of the groups to perform their role play for the class. Invite the class to feed back their opinions about how well they understood what was happening, how clear and audible the dialogue was and what persuasive features they recognised. Explain that the children are all going to perform their role plays in the next session, and that they will be recorded to become part of a multi-media ICT based presentation.	**Support:** work with some groups to help them improve dialogue

DAY 3 ■ Performing a persuasive role play

Key features	Stages	Additional opportunities

Introduction

Explain to the class that today they will perform their polished role-play persuasive scenes while you record them. Ensure to get parents' or carers' permission before recording the children. Tell the children that they will all be able to see each group's role play on screen at the end of the lesson.

Speaking and listening

Allow time for the children to rehearse and polish their performances before asking them to perform their role plays, one group at a time. Record the groups using a digital camera.

Independent work

While the groups are performing their role play, ask the rest of the children to write a short paragraph of three sentences to recount what part they played in their group's scene using the first person and past tense verbs.

Support: give children a sentence stem

Evaluation: give feedback and judge the effectiveness of their own work

Plenary

Put the recordings of the children's scenes onto a computer and play them to the class. Save them for use in their class ICT presentations.Discuss with the children how effective the role plays were when viewed on screen. Ask some of the children to read their three-sentence paragraphs aloud.

Guided reading

Select a recount non-fiction text at an appropriate level for the group. Identify first and third person verbs and past tense verbs. Discus the use of connectives to sequence a recount.

Assessment

Ask the children to summarise the features of persuasive texts they have learned in the Unit.
Observation: Do the children make contributions to the group while planning and performing the role play? Refer back to the learning outcomes on page 139.

Further work

Ask the children to improvise different scenes for their topic area.

DAY 1 ■ Plan a report

Key features	Stages	Additional opportunities
Enquiry: plan how to present information effectively	**Introduction** Review the task with the class. Remind them that they are going to produce a presentation of their research findings using different text types and ICT. Ask the children to suggest what different types of text they could use for the presentation. Draw up a list: non-chronological report, instructions, recount. Explain that you are going to focus on reports in this session. Ask the class to recall the key features of non-chronological reports. Discuss ways in which the information could be written. *Could it be an alphabetically-ordered text? Or should it be a report similar to the demonstration writing you did on Day 6 of Phase 1?* Remind the children of how you chose the topic and headings.	**Support:** provide copies of photocopiable page 118 'Reports' from Unit 1 to remind children about the structure of report text
	Speaking and listening Ask the groups to review the information they found on their topic and discuss how best to write it as a report. They should consider whether to use all the information or focus on one or two aspects.	
	Independent work Ask the children to use the Report skeleton from the CD-ROM to plan the organisation of their reports. Encourage them to create individual plans and then to share their ideas with their group.	**Extend:** some children can plan their reports without using the report skeleton
Evaluation: discuss success criteria	**Plenary** Ask some of the groups to share their plans with the class. Discuss success criteria with the class and draw up a list together.	

DAY 2 ■ Write a group report

Key features	Stages	Additional opportunities
	Introduction Explain that the children are going to spend more time writing today as they need to finish their reports. Some are going to be written using the computer and others on paper. The reports must be contributed to by each member of the group.	
Communication: work collaboratively in group contexts **Social skills:** when developing collaborative writing, learn to listen to and respect others' viewpoints and take on different roles to complete a task	**Speaking and listening** Ask the groups to spend no more than ten minutes to finalise their skeleton plans and then to divide the sections (introduction, subheadings and paragraphs, conclusion) between the group members. Ask the children to think about whether any of the sections will need illustrations or diagrams and to choose who will do these, so that each group member has a task.	
	Independent work Tell each member of the group to use the information in the relevant part of the skeleton to write a paragraph for the group's report. They should then regroup and read the report through. Tell them to cut and paste the individual pieces of writing onto one piece of paper.	**Extend:** some of the groups write their reports using computers
Evaluation: give feedback and judge effectiveness of own work	**Plenary** Ask some of the groups to read their completed reports aloud. Review the success criteria. Invite the children to feed back their opinions. Have the groups used the typical features of non-chronological reports? Are the individual sections ordered in a logical way?	

DAY 3 ▪ Instructions

Key features	Stages	Additional opportunities
	### Introduction Display the list of text types from Day 1 once more. Explain that you are going to focus on instructions in this session. Encourage the class to recall the key features of instruction texts. Discuss ways in which the information (answers to the groups' lists of questions) could be written as a set of instructions. Ask them to try to focus on different information from that which was used to write a report. Tell the children to recall what they have learned about the language features and layout of instructions.	**Speaking and listening:** work in pairs with the 'Around town' map from the CD-ROM; one child should ask the other for oral instructions on how to get from one specific place to another, finding safe places for crossing roads using the Green Cross Code
	### Speaking and listening Ask the groups to review the information on their topic again, and discuss which part of it could be written as a set of instructions. Tell them they will be writing the instructions in pairs.	
Communication: work collaboratively in pairs **Evaluation:** discuss success criteria, give feedback to others and judge effectiveness of their own work	### Independent work Encourage the pairs of children to use the Instruction skeleton from the CD-ROM to plan their writing, before writing the final version. ### Plenary Ask some of the pairs to share their instructions with the class. Compare the different topics they chose and discuss which ones make the most effective instructions.	**Support:** display photocopiable page 135 'Features of instruction texts' from Unit 2

DAY 4 ▪ Recount plans

Key features	Stages	Additional opportunities
	### Introduction Display the list of text types again. Explain that, in this session, the children are going to be writing part of their research as a recount. Ask for suggestions about which parts of their findings could be written as a recount. Suggest that they might like to write a first person recount of how they did their research, or to imagine someone has been involved in a part of the topic, for example what the school crossing-patrol person did one day, what a police officer wrote when reporting a speeding offence. Encourage the class to recall the key features of recounts. Ask them to try to focus on different information from that which was used to write a report or instructions if possible. Tell the children to recall what they have learned about the language features and layout of recounts.	
Enquiry: plan how to present information effectively	### Speaking and listening Ask the groups to discuss their ideas for the subject of their recounts. Tell them they will be writing their recounts individually.	**Support:** write their recount plans with a partner
Enquiry: plan how to present information effectively	### Independent work Let the children use the Recount skeleton from the CD-ROM to plan their writing, and to make brief notes in chronological order. ### Plenary Ask the children to use their skeleton notes to describe their recount to a partner, and to check that the order makes sense and that a consistent first or third person past tense is used. Discuss success criteria with the class.	

DAY 5 ■ Writing a recount

Key features	Stages	Additional opportunities
	Introduction Explain that the children are going to use their skeleton plans to write their recounts in this session. Some are going to be written using the computer and others on paper. Tell the children they should give a title to their work. Ask some children to say what the subject of their recount is and discuss possible titles. Remind the children to check their spelling and punctuation. Remind them also that they should use time-based words to help sequence the information. Brainstorm a list and display it for reference.	
Social skills: listen to and respect others' viewpoints	**Speaking and listening** Ask the children to work with a partner and to spend no more than ten minutes to discuss the skeleton plans and make any improvements needed.	
	Independent work Tell some of the children to use pen and paper to write their recounts and others to use a computer.	**ICT:** encourage different children from the previous sessions to write using computers
Evaluation: discuss success criteria, give feedback to others and judge the effectiveness of their own work	**Plenary** Review the success criteria with the class. Ask some of the children to read their completed recounts aloud. Ask the class to feed back their opinions. Have the children used the typical features of a recount, such as keeping a consistent point of view and using past tense verbs? Have they used time-based connectives to sequence the events described? Have they kept the details factual, and not told a story?	

DAY 6 ■ Creating an ICT presentation

Key features	Stages	Additional opportunities
	Introduction Remind the children of the outcome for this Unit of work, to create a collaborative ICT based presentation featuring different text types. Ask the children to recall what they have achieved so far in the Unit: researching specific answers to their own questions, designing and creating advertisements, making persuasive role-play videos, writing non-chronological reports, instructions and recounts. Explain that each group will be using ICT to collate their work and create a presentation on roads and road safety.	
Enquiry: plan how to present information effectively **Social skills:** take on different roles within a group to complete a task	**Speaking and listening** Encourage the groups to discuss how they should organise their work for an on-screen presentation. Should they present all the common text types one after another, in other words all the group's instructions followed by all the recounts; should they vary the order, should they display some as thumbnails and so on? Ask the children to discuss roles for this activity in their groups, and tell pairs of children to collect and scan paper-based work and save them on the computer. Remind them to collaborate with each other to copy, insert and save their work.	**Support:** work with groups who need help in creating and saving the presentation
	Plenary Discuss the children's expectations about how their presentations will look on screen as a slideshow.	

DAY 7 ■ Viewing the presentation

Key features	Stages	Additional opportunities
Enquiry: plan how to present information effectively	**Introduction** Tell the children they are to finish creating their slideshow presentations today and they will be able to watch each other's at the end of the session. Ask the children if there are any aspects of the task with which they need more help. **Independent work** Encourage the children to continue working in their groups to complete the presentations. Ask them to check their by viewing it at different stages of the process to see if the order makes sense, if anything is missing and if should they add any headings and subheadings to help viewers understand the content and so on. Allow time for the groups to polish their slideshow presentations.	**Support:** provide help to groups as necessary
Evaluation: present information orally and in writing; discuss success criteria, give feedback to others and judge the effectiveness of their own work	**Plenary** Discuss and agree success criteria for the final presentations, based on the success criteria for the stages of writing in this Unit. Play each group's slideshow presentation to the class. Take feedback about what the children have achieved and which areas need further work. You could upload their presentations onto the school or local website.	

Guided reading

Select recounts, instruction texts and non-chronological reports at an appropriate level. Work with groups to support them in consolidating the features of each of the text types.

Assessment

Self-assessment against agreed success criteria.
Teacher observation: Do the children differentiate between the different types of text they have been writing and creating?
Children complete the CD-ROM assessment activity 'Labels'.
Refer back to the learning outcomes on page 139.

Further work

Provide examples of the featured non-fiction texts and encourage independent reading.

KWL Chart

What I KNOW	What I WANT to know	What I have LEARNED

Questions

◼ Rewrite these questions. Add capital letters and the correct punctuation.

1. where is a safe place to cross the road

_____

2. what is your name

_____

3. how slowly can you ride your bike

_____

4. can you ride your bike yet

_____

5. why did you run over the road

_____

6. who is driving the car

_____

PHOTOCOPIABLE ◼ SCHOLASTIC
www.scholastic.co.uk

Persuasion

Persuasive texts can be:

Advertisements

Posters

Leaflets

Newspapers

Television

Layout

Statements

Rhetorical questions

Headings

Subheadings

Photographs

Diagrams

Captions

Labels

Language features

Present tense verbs

Imperative verbs

Second person verbs 'you'

Third person verbs 'we'

Specific examples

Connectives to compare and contrast

Persuasive texts tell us _why_ we should think or act in a certain way

Advertising

1. What are you selling? Think of a name for it.

2. Ask a question.

3. Write a sentence about how good it is.

4. Write a sentence about why people need it.

5. Ask another question.

6. Where can people get it from? Give an instruction.

POETRY
UNIT 1 Poems to perform

Speak and listen for a range of purposes on paper and on screen

Strand 1 Speaking
- Choose and prepare poems or stories for performance, identifying appropriate expression, tone, volume and use of voices and other sounds.

Strand 3 Group discussion and interaction
- Actively include and respond to all members of the group.

Strand 4 Drama
- Identify and discuss qualities of others' performances, including gesture, action, costume.

Read for a range of purposes on paper and on screen

Strand 6 Word structure and Spelling
- Spell high and medium frequency words.

Strand 7 Understanding and interpreting texts
- Explore how different texts appeal to readers using varied sentence structures and descriptive language.

Strand 8 Engaging with and responding to texts
- Identify features that writers use to provoke readers' reactions.

Write for a range of purposes on paper and on screen

Strand 10 Text structure and organisation
- Signal sequence, place and time to give coherence.

Strand 11 Sentence structure and punctuation
- Show relationships of time, reason and cause through, subordination and connectives.

Strand 12 Presentation
- Write with consistency in size and proportion of letters and spacing within and between words, using the correct formation of handwriting joins.
- Develop accuracy and speed when using keyboard skills to type, edit and re-draft.

Progression in poetry

In this year children are moving towards:
- Describing the effect a poem has and suggesting possible interpretations.
- Discussing the choice of words and their impact, noticing how the poet creates 'sound effects' by using alliteration, rhythm or rhyme and creates pictures using similes.
- Explaining the pattern of different simple forms.
- Performing individually or chorally; varying volume, experimenting with expression and using pauses for effect.
- Using actions, voices, sound effects and musical patterns to add to a performance.
- Inventing new similes and experimenting with word play.
- Using powerful nouns, adjectives and verbs; experimenting with alliteration.
- Writing free verse; borrowing or creating a repeating pattern.

Key aspects of learning covered in this Unit

Self-awareness
Children will discuss and reflect on their personal responses to poems read.

Creative thinking
Children will use creative thinking to extend and consider alternatives to simple poetic forms and create a new poem of their own.

Evaluation
Children will give feedback to others and judge the effectiveness of their own descriptions.

Social skills
When working collaboratively, children will listen to and respect other people's ideas. They will undertake a variety of roles in group contexts.

Prior learning

Before starting this Unit check that the children can:
■ Talk about their own views; discuss patterns in poetry; perform individually or with others using a clear audible voice.
If they need further support please refer to a prior Unit or a similar Unit in Year 2.

Resources

Phase 1:
Conversation at the school dinner table by John Rice ✿; *Heads or tails?* by Kit Wright ✿; Poetry anthologies
Phase 2:
Black Dot by Libby Houston ✿; *Fish* by Gillian Howell ✿; Thesaurus; Photocopiable page 166 'My list poem'; Poetry anthologies
Phase 3:
Heads or tails? by Kit Wright ✿; Photocopiable page 167 'Alliterative animals'; Photocopiable page 168 'Poem planning'; Rhyming dictionaries – print or on screen; Thesaurus; Poetry anthologies; Assessment activity 'Rhyme or alliteration' ✿

Cross-curricular opportunities

Drama

UNIT 1 ■ Teaching sequence

Phase	Children's objectives	Summary of activities	Learning outcomes
1	I can use an expressive voice.	Shared reading of a poem and annotating its language features. Read alternate verses aloud in pairs and in groups.	Children can explain their opinions about a poem by referring to particular words and phrases and the subject of the poem.
	I can perform a poem.	Shared reading of a poem. Discuss a performance of the poem in groups. Group performance.	Children can identify where language is used to create an effect.
2	I can enact a poem.	Shared reading of a poem. Group performance using movement and gesture.	
	I can write a list poem.	Modelled writing of a kenning. Write a poem independently.	Children can write a poem that uses language to create an effect.
3	I can begin a draft.	Shared reading of a poem. Modelled writing. Brainstorm ideas and begin a draft.	
	I can write and perform poetry.	Collaborate to finalise, rehearse and perform their poems.	

Provide copies of the objectives for the children.

DAY 1 ■ Conversational poetry

Key features	Stages	Additional opportunities
	### Introduction Explain to the children that they are going to be reading and performing poetry together. Ask the children to describe their favourite poems or one that they are familiar with. Display the poem *Conversation at the school dinner table* from the CD-ROM. Hide the poem, leaving only the title showing and read this to the class. Ask the children to predict what they think might be in this poem. Reveal the poem and read it aloud, emphasising the conversational style and the nonsense words. Ask them to give their opinions about the poem. What is funny about it? Re-read it more slowly with the children following the lines. Annotate the poem, identifying the verses, who is speaking (three or possibly four children) and the repeated patterns of the nonsense words. Ask some of the children to read the nonsense words aloud. Re-read the poem with the whole class joining in.	**HFW:** could, what, want, over, do, don't, with
Social skills: working collaboratively	### Speaking and listening Give the children copies of the poem. Ask them to work with a partner and read alternate verses aloud to each other. Encourage them to use expressive voices as if the conversation is real.	**Support:** break the nonsense words into syllables to help children read them **Extend:** rewrite the poem as a narrative conversation with speech punctuation
	### Plenary Agree as a class how many speakers feature in the poem. Divide the class into the same number of groups and read the poem aloud, each group reading the verses of one speaker.	

DAY 2 ■ Performing in a group

Key features	Stages	Additional opportunities
Communication: work collaboratively in group and whole-class contexts	### Introduction Display the poem *Heads or tails?* from the CD-ROM. Read it aloud to the class, and ask the children to describe what they think the poem is about. Ask them to suggest why it is called *Heads or tails?* Re-read it, emphasising rhythm, rhyme and alliteration. Ask the children to identify the rhyming words and mark them on the poem. Encourage the children what they notice about the rhymes and the verses. Elicit that each verse has its own rhyme scheme and they are different. Ask them why the author has used italic print (emphasis). Focus on verse two and ask the class to work out how many speakers there are. Ask for eight volunteers to read verse two aloud, with you taking 'Somebody said' and each child reading one set of spoken words. Encourage expressive voices. Focus on the last two lines of verse three, and tell the children to find the alliterative words. Ask them to find these lines somewhere else in the poem (verse one). Invite the children to identify the punctuation that defines each sentence. What do they notice about verse three? (It is one sentence.) Do they think that Dave's dog is really horrible?	**MFW:** first, brought, round, inside, knows, clothes
Social skills: listen to and respect other people's opinions	### Speaking and listening Give groups of children copies of the poem and ask them to discuss how best to perform it. Should they read the poem chorally, using alternate verses or taking separate sentences?	**Extend:** encourage the children to add actions and gestures to their performance
	### Independent work Ask the groups to perform the poem to the class. Discuss their chosen methods.	

Guided reading

Provide the group with a different performance poem at an appropriate level. Identify rhyme, rhythm and alliteration. Encourage the children to read the poem aloud, emphasising the rhythm.

Assessment

Observation: Do the children contribute to group discussion and performance?

Are the children making use of the rhythm to perform the poem aloud?

Can the children use appropriate terms to describe poetry?

Refer back to the learning outcomes on page 159.

Further work

Ask the children to read anthologies of poetry to identify poems suitable for performance and give reasons for their opinions.

Provide other poems for performance with strong rhythms and ask groups to read aloud in expressive voices.

Give the children one or two specific poetic features, for example rhyme and alliteration, and ask them to identify examples in other poems.

DAY 1 ■ List poem

Key features	Stages	Additional opportunities

Introduction
Display the poem *Black Dot* from the CD-ROM. Ask the children to study the layout of the poem and describe how it looks. Elicit that it is a long thin poem with few words. Read the poem to the class. Ask the children to suggest what the poem is about. Explain that it is a *kenning*, which is a list poem that uses two words in each line to describe something. Point out that the poem is a list of what makes a frog, beginning with a black dot (frog spawn) and ending with an adult frog. Re-read it and emphasise the rhyming couplets and the final rhyme (*catalogue/frog*).

MFW: high, black, eyes, swimmer

Support: use the poem *Fish* from the CD-ROM

Creative thinking: respond imaginatively to a stimulus

Speaking and listening
Ask the class to perform the poem while you read it aloud. Tell them they are not going to use their voices, but to make actions and gestures to suit each line. Before beginning, encourage them to take a few minutes to discuss what sort of actions and movements they could do, and whether there are any lines that cannot be interpreted by movement. Read the poem while the children make suitable movements or gestures.

Independent work
Provide the children with copies of the poem. Ask the children to read the poem with a partner, taking alternate lines. Encourage them to think of how to perform the poem.

Plenary
Gather the children together and discuss options for performing the poem. Ask them to give opinions on the effectiveness of using movement.

DAY 2 ■ Writing a list poem

Key features	Stages	Additional opportunities

Introduction
Explain that the children are going to write their own kenning style list poems about themselves. Model how to write a two word line about yourself using a noun-verb pattern, for example *book-lover*, *dog walker*. Write a list of a few things that define you: job, hobbies, appearance and so on. Demonstrate how to think of a two-word phrase for each thing on your list. Now ask some of the children about the things they do and look like, such as *play football*, *dance*, *ride a bike*, and their appearance, for example *wear trainers*, *jeans*. Model how to turn some into noun-verb phrases, such as *jeans-wearer*, *bike-rider*. Emphasise that they do not need to worry about making them rhyme, but they can if they wish to, for example *sandwich-maker*, *record-breaker*.

Extend: look for more interesting vocabulary using a thesaurus

Self-awareness: discuss reflect on their personal responses

Speaking and listening
Encourage the children to discuss their hobbies, activities and appearances with a partner and help each other draw up a list of nouns.

Support: use photocopiable page 166 'My list poem'; you might want to delete the sample phrases for some children

Evaluation: give feedback to others and judge effectiveness of their own descriptions

Independent work
Ask the children to write an eight line list poem about themselves.

Plenary
Invite the children to read their list poems aloud. Ask them to give their opinions on the effectiveness of the poems, for example which children have used unusual combinations of words.

Guided reading

Provide the group with anthologies that include list poems and kennings. Encourage the children to identify patterns and rhythm.

Assessment

Observation: Do the children understand and respond to different types of rhythm when reading a poem?

Can they write a two word phrase using a noun-verb combination?

Can they write a list poem about themselves?

Peer assessment: Are the children able to discuss and evaluate each other's list poems?

Refer back to the learning outcomes on page 159.

Further work

Ask children who used photocopiable page 166 'My list poem' with the phrase prompts to write another list poem about a friend without the prompts. They can then discuss the poems in pairs.

DAY 1 ◼ Borrowing patterns

Key features	Stages	Additional opportunities
Reasoning: explain their opinions using particular words and phrases	### Introduction Explain that the children will be writing their own performance poems by borrowing some of the poetic features they have explored in this Unit. Ask the children to suggest the language features they could use and draw up a list on the board, for example alliteration, rhythm, repetition. Read the poem *Heads or tails?* from the CD-ROM to the class once more. Display the poem and ask the children to focus on the first two lines. Annotate the text to identify the alliteration in line one: *Dave Dirt's dog – horrible hound,* and the a/b rhyme scheme. Model how to borrow ideas from the poem by thinking of an alliterative name and animal, for example *Caroline's cat, Henry's horse.* Demonstrate your thought processes aloud (*What could Caroline's cat be like – nice or nasty?*) and write examples on the board: *Caroline's cat was a mangy mutt. Henry's horse was a marvellous mare*, and so on.	
	### Independent work Ask the children to work in groups and brainstorm ideas for a poem they will write and perform based on the poems studied in the Unit. Ask them to begin drafting the poem using rhyming dictionaries, in print and on screen, and a thesaurus.	**Support:** use an example from the whole-class session or use photocopiable page 167 'Alliterative animals'
	### Plenary Take feedback from the children about how they are progressing and discuss any difficulties they have met. Ask some of the groups to read their opening lines.	

DAY 2 ◼ Writing a poem

Key features	Stages	Additional opportunities
	### Introduction Using the opening line from the poem you modelled in the previous session, demonstrate how to count the beats and ask the children to clap the rhythm. Discuss why this is important in this poem. Demonstrate how to add more lines with the same or similar beat, for example: *Henry's horse was a marvellous mare* *as everybody saw/knew.* *When she jumped she flew in the air* *and everyone cried 'cor!'/'ooh!'* Remind the children about the task – to write and perform their own poems in groups.	**Support:** focus on using a simpler a/b a/c rhyme scheme; use photocopiable page 168 'Poem planning' to help them plan their poem
Social skills: work collaboratively; listen to and respect other people's ideas	### Speaking and listening Ask the groups to collaborate with each other to continue their own poems, sharing ideas and helping to find rhymes. Let them finish and rehearse the performance of their poem.	
	### Plenary Invite each group to perform their poem for the class. Discuss and compare the poems and performances. Ask the children to evaluate the poems and each group member's contributions and give reasons for their opinions.	

Guided reading

Provide poetry anthologies and ask the children to select and read a poem with a strong rhythm. Ask them to clap the rhythm as they read.

Assessment

Peer assessment: Children evaluate each other's poems.

Observation: Do the children recognise words which rhyme?

Are the children able to 'hear' and recreate a poem's rhythm?

Do the children understand and use alliteration?

Children can complete the CD-ROM assessment activity 'Rhyme or alliteration'.

Refer back to the learning outcomes on page 159.

Further work

Ask children to add another verse to their poems.

My list poem

■ Use the prompts to help you describe yourself in a six line list poem. You can use the phrases at the bottom to help you.

Two words to describe your face _____

Two words about a colour _____

Two words about your clothes _____

Two words about food _____

Two words about a game _____

Two words about a hobby _____

and that...

adds up...

to

Who are you? _____

smile-giver   red-wearer   game-player   ball-bouncer
uniform-hater   picture-painter nose-blower   blue-hater
pizza-eater   eye-blinker   fleece-wearer   bean-grower
judo-thrower

 ■ 100 LITERACY FRAMEWORK LESSONS YEAR 3   **PHOTOCOPIABLE** ■SCHOLASTIC
www.scholastic.co.uk

Alliterative animals

■ Choose words from the lists of animals to make alliterative phrases.

Ben's _____

Jack's _____

Harry's _____

Carly's _____

Dave's _____

Mark's _____

| cat | badger | gerbil | donkey | mouse | hedgehog |

Poem planning

■ Use the chart to help you plan your poem. Experiment with different alliterative phrases.

a name	an animal	a verb	adjective	noun		
Brenda's	budgie	ate	bendy	bananas		

PHOTOCOPIABLE ■SCHOLASTIC
www.scholastic.co.uk

POETRY
UNIT 2 Shape poems and calligrams

Speak and listen for a range of purposes on paper and on screen

Strand 1 Speaking
■ Sustain conversation, explain or give reasons for their views or choices.

Read for a range of purposes on paper and on screen

Strand 7 Understanding and interpreting texts
■ Explore how different texts appeal to readers using varied sentence structures and descriptive language.
Strand 8 Engaging with and responding to texts
■ Identify features that writers use to provoke readers' reactions.

Write for a range of purposes on paper and on screen

Strand 9 Creating and shaping texts
■ Select and use a range of technical and descriptive vocabulary.
■ Use layout, format, graphics and illustrations for different purposes.
Strand 11 Sentence structure and punctuation
■ Compose sentences using adjectives, verbs and nouns for precision, clarity and impact.
Strand 12 Presentation
■ Write with a consistency in the size and proportion of letters and spacing within and between words, using the correct formation of handwriting joins.
■ Develop accuracy and speed when using keyboard skills to type, edit and re-draft.

Progression in poetry

In this year children are moving towards:
■ Describing the effect a poem has and suggesting possible interpretations.
■ Discussing the choice of words and their impact, noticing how the poet creates 'sound effects' by using alliteration, rhythm or rhyme and creates pictures using similes.
■ Explaining the pattern of different simple forms.
■ Inventing new similes and experimenting with word play.
■ Using powerful nouns, adjectives and verbs; experiment with alliteration.
■ Borrowing or creating a repeating pattern.

UNIT 2 ◀ Shape poems and calligrams *continued*

Key aspects of learning covered in this Unit

Reasoning
Children will explain their opinion about different poems, using particular words and phrases to support or illustrate their ideas.

Creative thinking
Children will have the opportunity to respond imaginatively to the stimulus of a first-hand experience and may be able to express their response through music, art or dance before writing poems.

Evaluation
Children will have regular opportunities to review their written work against agreed success criteria.

Prior learning

Before starting this Unit check that the children can:
■ Compare and contrast different poems discussing preferences and referring to words or phrases in the text.
If they need further support please refer to a prior Unit or a similar Unit in Year 2.

Resources

Phase 1:
Autumn by Tony Langham ❀; *Orange* by John Cotton ❀; *Pineapple* by John Cotton ❀; *Holiday memories* by Paula Edwards ❀; Photocopiable page 178 'The best poem'; Photocopiable page 179 'Calligrams'; Computer access, with word-processing software; Poetry anthology with shape poems and calligrams

Phase 2:
Photograph of a cup and saucer ❀; Photograph of a snail ❀; Photograph of a shark ❀; Photograph of a snake ❀

Phase 3:
Digital photographs suitable for shape poetry stimulus; *Autumn* by Tony Langham ❀; *Orange* by John Cotton ❀; *Pineapple* by John Cotton ❀; Photocopiable page 180 'Snail shape'; Assessment activity 'Shape poems' ❀

Cross-curricular opportunities

ICT
Art
Drama

UNIT 2 ■ Teaching sequence

Phase	Children's objectives	Summary of activities	Learning outcomes
1	I can read and compare poems.	Shared reading of shape poems and calligrams. Write sentences describing their opinions.	Children can explain what they like about a poem by referring to particular words and phrases and the subject of the poem.
	I can write a calligram.	Shared writing of calligrams. Create their own calligrams on paper and on computer.	Children can write a calligram, choosing appropriate presentational features using ICT to create effects, and can describe why these effects have been chosen.
2	I can create poetic words and phrases.	Class discussion on words and images. Role play the images and create similes.	Children can identify examples where language is used to create a specific effect in a poem.
	I can contribute to a class poem.	Shared writing of a shape poem. Plan using patterned language	Children can discuss the choice of words and their impact.
3	I can create a shape poem.	Create an outline shape and brainstorm associated words and phrases.	
		Polish and complete their individual shape poems.	Children can write a poem (collaboratively or individually) that uses language to create an effect.

Provide copies of the objectives for the children.

DAY 1 ■ Shapes

Key features	Stages	Additional opportunities
Reasoning: explain their opinions about different poems, using particular words and phrases to support or illustrate their ideas	**Introduction** Explain that the class will be looking at different ways of writing poetry using shapes as a stimulus. Display the poem *Autumn* from the CD-ROM. Before reading it, ask the children what they think it looks like. Ask them to decide where you should begin reading and then read the poem. Display *Orange* from the CD-ROM, without showing the title. Ask the children what they think the subject of the poem is and why. Read the poem. Next display *Pineapple* from the CD-ROM and ask what the subject is. Encourage the children to say how similar and different the three poems are. Invite them to say which poem is most effective visually. Which poem do they prefer? Discuss why the poets have chosen these shapes, and how the shape affects the content of the poems. Display the poem *Holiday memories* from the CD-ROM. Before reading, ask the children what they immediately notice about this poem. Read the poem to the children. Tell them that the first three poems were shape poetry but this is a calligram. Ask the children how this poem differs from the previous poems. Elicit that the shape of the subject inspires the poem in shape poetry, but the meaning of words inspires the shapes in a calligram.	**MFW:** leaves, start
	Independent work Ask the children to choose which poem they preferred and write three sentences explaining why. Explain that there is no right or wrong answer.	**Support:** use photocopiable page 178 'The best poem' to help them
	Plenary Compare and contrast the children's choices and reasons for preferences.	

DAY 2 ■ Writing a calligram

Key features	Stages	Additional opportunities
	Introduction Display the poem *Holiday memories* from the CD-ROM and analyse with the children how the poet has illustrated and shaped the words to reflect their meaning. Ask the children to suggest some other adjectives and collaborate with them in writing them by hand on the board in different ways to reflect meaning. Use a word-processing program to write the adjectives and demonstrate how to shape and change the words. Encourage the children to discuss the results and whether it is easier to write them by hand or on a computer. Save the results and display the computer generated words and the handwritten ones for comparison. Choose one of the adjectives and demonstrate how to make a movement or action to act it out, for example *cold* – make an exaggerated, shivering movement.	
Creative thinking: respond imaginatively	**Speaking and listening** Call out adjectives one by one and ask the children to act them out through movement and gesture.	
	Independent work Encourage some of the children to work in pairs and create calligrams using a computer, and some to create them by hand.	**Support:** use photocopiable page 179 'Calligrams'
	Plenary Show the calligrams to the class. Discuss and compare how similar or different their interpretations are, how they manipulated fonts, size and so on. Compare handwritten calligrams with the computer generated ones.	

Guided reading

Provide the group with a poetry anthology containing shape poems and calligrams. Read two or three by different poets and compare how they have used shapes to reflect meaning. Ask the children to state their preferences and reasons for their opinions.

Assessment

Observation: Can the children explain how they created their calligrams and describe the effect they wanted to create?

Refer back to the learning outcomes on page 171.

Further work

Ask children who created handwritten calligrams to use a computer to create others, and vice versa.

DAY 1 ▪ Images and impressions

Key features	Stages	Additional opportunities
Creative thinking: respond imaginatively	**Introduction** Display the photographs of the snail, shark, cup and saucer and snake from the CD-ROM. Focus on one at a time. Ask the children what the image is, what they know about it and how it makes them feel. Ask them to say a word associated with each image. Concentrate on aspects of interest and brainstorm other words associated with them. Collect the children's suggestions as a list. Remind the children about similes and give them an example for one of the images, for example *snail – shiny as a snail trail*.	
Creative thinking: express their response before writing	**Speaking and listening** Call out the name of the images one at a time and ask the children to act it out, for example *snake – children slither as if they were snakes*. Call out some of the associated words and ask the children to interpret them through movement. Return to the photographs from the CD-ROM and ask the children to suggest words and phrases as a result of their role-play activity.	
	Independent work Ask the children to work with a partner and create a simile for each image.	**Support:** provide a writing frame: _____ as a _____ _____ like a _____
	Plenary Ask the children to share their similes and add them to the brainstormed list on the board.	

DAY 2 ▪ A class shape poem

Key features	Stages	Additional opportunities
	Introduction Display the photographs from the CD-ROM again. Select one of the images as a stimulus and ask the children, in pairs, to use individual whiteboards to write two adjectives or a simile. Discuss their ideas and select some of them for use for a class shape poem. Ask the children to suggest which words and phrases could be used for a repeated pattern in their poem. Draw an outline of the chosen image on the board and explain that this will be the shape that contains the poem. Collaborate with the children to write the selected adjectives, phrases and similes onto the chosen image in a random order.	**Support:** write one adjective
	Independent work Ask the children to work with their partners, and experiment with re-ordering and regrouping the selected words and phrases to develop a poem that uses repetition of these words and phrases. Discuss and collect the children's ideas and collaborate to create a class shape poem together. Demonstrate how to write the class poem inside the outline.	
Evaluation: review work	**Plenary** Remove the outline from the board, retaining the shape poem and explore the shape made by the words alone. Discuss the effect.	

Guided writing

Use shape poems, such as those from Phase 1, and support the group to write their own shape poems using these as outlines. Focus on using imaginative adjectives and similes.

Assessment

Observation: Do the children understand the term *simile*? Can they make comparisons to create imaginative effects?
Self assessment: are they choosing words that will make an impact? Refer back to the learning outcomes on page 171.

Further work

Select other poems, including shape poetry, and ask the children to identify similes and write them in their personal writing journals or word books.

DAY 1 ■ Planning a shape poem

Key features	Stages	Additional opportunities
	Introduction Provide a selection of digital photographs for the children to use. Explain that they are going to write their own shape poems using a digital photograph. Discuss and agree success criteria appropriate to the children's targets. Together, look through the photographs and explore language as a stimulus to generate their own ideas.	
Creative thinking: respond imaginatively	**Speaking and listening** Provide pairs of children with a photograph and ask them to talk together about it, how they feel about it and their memories or experiences associated with it. Encourage them to brainstorm words and phrases to use for a poem on the subject.	**Extend:** create and draw a shape from their own imaginations **Support:** use photocopiable page 180 'Snail shape' to make notes of associations, memories, words and phrases
	Independent work Ask the pairs of children to make brief notes of their ideas associated with the shape of their image. Provide each child with tracing paper and ask them to draw an outline shape over the image to use for writing their shape poem.	
Evaluation: review work against success criteria	**Plenary** Ask some of the pairs of children to tell the rest of the class about their image and their ideas for creating a poem. Discuss and praise their use of simile and poetic language.	

DAY 2 ■ Writing a shape poem

Key features	Stages	Additional opportunities
	Introduction Display the shape poems *Autumn, Orange* and *Pineapple* from the CD-ROM. Re-read them together. Explain that the children will be writing their own poems using the shape they explored yesterday. Tell them to use the notes from their paired work in the previous session. Encourage the children to draft and improve their ideas independently on a separate piece of paper. Ask them each to write the polished version into the shape of their image. Provide them with their image from the previous lesson.	
Reasoning: explain their opinions about different poems	**Independent work** Tell the children to work with their response partners as they write their own individual poems. They should compare each other's ideas, make suggestions for editing and improving and support each other as they work.	**Extend:** play with the shapes of words within their shape poems to create the effects of calligrams
Evaluation: review work against success criteria and personal targets	**Plenary** Make a display of all the children's poems. Invite the children to read them and comment on the effect of the layout and poetic language. Ask the children to express their personal opinions about the poems, supporting their reasons with evidence. Review the success criteria for the task and consider whether the children have achieved their targets. Ask them if there are areas where they need further help in order to progress towards the targets.	

Guided writing

Support groups in writing a group shape poem. Encourage and help them to create and select imaginative and thoughtful phrases.

Assessment

Peer assessment: Identify examples where language is used to create a specific effect in their own poem and in others' poems.

Discuss progress towards agreed success criteria.

Children can complete the CD-ROM assessment activity 'Shape poem'. Refer back to the learning outcomes on page 171.

Further work

Ask the children to use art to improve the presentation and impact of their shape poems for a class display.

The best poem

■ Write about the poem you like best.

The poem I like best is called _____

_____

I like it because the shape is _____

_____

Another reason is that it made me feel _____

_____

Add a sentence of your own _____

_____

■ Draw a picture of your poem.

■ 100 LITERACY FRAMEWORK LESSONS YEAR 3

PHOTOCOPIABLE ■SCHOLASTIC
www.scholastic.co.uk

Name _____   **Date** _____

Calligrams

■ Write your own calligram for these words. The first one has been done for you.

bendy

flat

shaky

prickly

soft

POETRY ■ UNIT 2

Snail shape

■ Use the snail to create your own shape poem.

■ 100 LITERACY FRAMEWORK LESSONS YEAR 3

Illustration © Nova Developments.

PHOTOCOPIABLE ■ SCHOLASTIC
www.scholastic.co.uk

POETRY
UNIT 3 Language play

Speak and listen for a range of purposes on paper and on screen

Strand 1 Speaking
- Choose and prepare poems or stories for performance, identifying appropriate expression, tone, volume and use of voices and other sounds.
- Sustain conversation, explain or give reasons for their views or choices.

Read for a range of purposes on paper and on screen

Strand 6 Word structure and spelling
- Spell high and medium frequency words.
- Recognise a range of prefixes and suffixes, understanding how they modify meaning and spelling, and how they assist in decoding long, complex words.
- Spell unfamiliar words using known conventions including phoneme/grapheme correspondence and morphological rules.

Strand 7 Understanding and interpreting texts
- Explore how different texts appeal to readers using varied sentence structures and descriptive language.

Strand 8 Engaging and responding to texts
- Identify features that writers use to provoke readers' reactions.

Write for a range of purposes on paper and on screen

Strand 9 Creating and shaping texts
- Make decisions about form and purpose, and identify success criteria for their writing.
- Use layout, format graphics and illustrations for different purposes.

Strand 11 Sentence structure and punctuation
- Compose sentences using adjectives, verbs and nouns for precision, clarity and impact.

Strand 12 Presentation
- Write with consistency in size and proportion of letters and spacing within and between words, using the correct formation of handwriting joins.
- Develop accuracy and speed when using keyboard skills to type, edit and re-draft.

Progression in poetry

In this year children are moving towards:
- Describing the effect a poem has and suggesting possible interpretations.
- Discussing the choice of words and their impact, noticing how the poet creates 'sound effects' by using alliteration, rhythm or rhyme and creates pictures using similes.
- Explaining the pattern of different simple forms.
- Performing individually or chorally; varying volume, experimenting with expression and using pauses for effect.
- Inventing new similes and experimenting with word play.
- Using powerful nouns, adjectives and verbs; experimenting with alliteration.
- Writing free verse; borrowing or creating a repeating pattern.

▶

UNIT 3 ◄ Language play *continued*

Key aspects of learning covered in this Unit

Reasoning
Children will be explaining their opinions about different poems and using particular words and phrases to support or illustrate their ideas.

Creative thinking
Children will have the opportunity to respond imaginatively to a stimulus of first hand experience and may be able to express their response through music, art or dance before writing poems.

Evaluation
Children will have regular opportunities to review their written work against agreed success criteria.

Communication
Children will develop their ability to discuss aspects of poetry and poetic language as they work collaboratively in paired, group and whole class contexts. They will communicate outcomes orally, in writing and through ICT if appropriate.

Prior learning

Before starting this Unit check that the children can:
■ Compare and contrast different poems discussing preferences and referring to words or phrases in the text.
If they need further support please refer to a prior Unit or a similar Unit in Year 2.

Resources

Phase 1:
The ghost house by John Foster ❦; *An attempt at unrhymed verse* by Wendy Cope ❦; *Don't put your finger in the jelly, Nelly!* by Nick Sharratt ❦; Photocopiable page 190 'To rhyme or not to rhyme'; Rhyming dictionary

Phase 2:
The Tutor by Carolyn Wells ❦; *A Fly and a Flea in a Flue* by Anon ❦; *Little Miss Muffet; Georgie Porgie; Hickory, Dickory, Dock* all by Dick King-Smith ❦; Photocopiable page 191 'Silly rhymes'; Photocopiable page 192 'Incy Wincy Spider'; Other humorous poems; Dictionaries

Phase 3:
Rainbow by David Whitehead ❦; *Poetry* by Gillian Howell ❦; Slideshow software and computer access; Assessment activity 'Snowdrop' ❦

Cross-curricular opportunities

ICT

UNIT 3 ■ Teaching sequence

Phase	Children's objectives	Summary of activities	Learning outcomes
1	I can contribute to a group performance.	Shared reading of a poem. Rehearse in groups and perform the poem.	Children can explain what they like about a poem by referring to particular words and phrases and the subject of the poem.
	I can write rhyming and unrhyming couplets.	Shared reading of a poem. Explore language play and write their own poems using a template.	Children can identify where language is used to create a specific effect in a poem.
2	I can write alliterative phrases.	Shared reading of tongue twisters. Groups create their own tongue twisters using alliteration.	
	I can play with words.	Shared reading and writing of new versions of nursery rhymes. Write a new version of a nursery rhyme.	Children can discuss the choice of words and their impact.
3	I can generate ideas for acrostic poems.	Shared reading and writing of an acrostic poem. Brainstorm ideas and begin a draft poem in groups and then in pairs.	Children can write a poem (collaboratively or individually) that uses language to create an effect.
	I can write an acrostic poem on screen.	Modelled writing. Complete their acrostic poems and write them on screen in pairs.	

Provide copies of the objectives for the children.

DAY 1 ■ Ghost house

Key features	Stages	Additional opportunities
	### Introduction	**Word-level:** focus on consonant clusters: fl/scr/tch/cl/nk, changing vowel sounds in flutter, scratch, rattle
Reasoning: explain their opinion about poems, using words and phrases to support their ideas	Remind the children about how they manipulated words to create shape poems and calligrams. Explain that they will be looking at other ways of manipulating words and language to create different poetic effects and ways of playing with language. Display the poem *The ghost house* from the CD-ROM. Read it to the children, emphasising the sound effects. Ask the children for their responses. Was it scary? Was it funny? Which aspects of the language did they enjoy? Re-read the poem and point out the surprise ending, and how the poet has combined onomatopoeia and font effects to convey the sounds. Remind the children about the performance poetry they read, and discuss whether *The ghost house* would make a good performance poem and why.	
Communication: develop ability to discuss aspects of poetry while working collaboratively in groups	### Speaking and listening Ask the children to work in groups and discuss how they think the poem should be performed. Tell them to consider if it should be performed by pairs or groups, chorally or taking roles. Allow time for the groups to rehearse the poem and then to perform it for the class.	**Support:** divide the poem so that some children read the repeated rhyming couplets and others the verses about sounds
	### Plenary Discuss and compare the ways different groups chose to perform *The ghost house*. Explain that the children will be writing their own poems that play with language at the end of the Unit. Discuss and agree success criteria with the children.	

DAY 2 ■ To rhyme or not to rhyme

Key features	Stages	Additional opportunities
	### Introduction	
Reasoning: explain their opinion about poems, using words and phrases to support their ideas	Display the poem *An attempt at unrhymed verse* from the CD-ROM. Mask the words *pencil, gherkins* and *the way you want it*. Read it to the children and invite them to join in and fill in the gaps. Encourage them to use obvious rhymes. Ask the children for their opinions about the poem. *Is it funny? Does it play with words?* Reveal the hidden words and re-read the poem to the children. Ask them if their opinions about the poem have changed. Explain how the poet has written the poem in a way that makes you predict the rhymes, but used unrhyming words instead to create a funny effect. Read the poem together, emphasising the rhythm and identify how the non-rhyming words affect it. Display *Don't put your finger in the jelly, Nelly!* from the CD-ROM. Read it to the children and ask them to identify the rhyming words. How is it different from the other rhyming poems? Ask them to identify the invented words and express their opinions of the effect.	
Creative thinking: respond imaginatively and express their response through writing	### Independent work Provide children with copies of photocopiable page 190 'To rhyme or not to rhyme'. Tell them to choose words for the couplets so that first they rhyme, and then so that they do *not* rhyme. Ask the children to discuss their choices with a partner and try to choose really unusual things.	**Support:** choose only rhyming words using a rhyming dictionary
	### Plenary Ask the children to read their rhyming and unrhyming versions. Compare the differences and how their choices of unrhymed words affected the rhythm.	

Guided reading

Read *The ghost house* with guided groups. Support the children in identifying onomatopoeic words. Discuss and write other words where sounds reflect meanings.

Assessment

Observation: Do the children contribute to group discussion and performance?

Can children differentiate between rhyming and unrhyming lines of poetry?

Do children understand how some words sound like their meaning?

Refer back to the learning outcomes on page 183.

Further work

Ask the children to write their own onomatopoeic phrases.

Suggest children find onomatopoeic rhymes, for example *splutter, flutter.*

DAY 1 ◾ Tongue twisters

Key features	Stages	Additional opportunities
Reasoning: explain their opinion about poems, using words and phrases to support their ideas	### Introduction Explain that you are going to look at other ways that poets create humour by playing with words. Display *The Tutor* and *A Fly and a Flea in a Flue* from the CD-ROM. Explain that these poems are difficult to say quickly. Ask the children to read the poems slowly out loud. Discuss what caused the children problems in reading. Identify the alliteration in each poem, the repetition of the long vowel sounds in *The Tutor* and the homophones in *A Fly and a Flea in a Flue*. Discuss how these create a humorous effect. Explain that these are called *tongue twisters* and talk about other tongue twisters the children may know, such as *Round and round the rugged rocks*. Explain that the children are going to make group tongue twisters based on their names as in *Peter Piper picked a peck of pickled pepper*.	
Communication: work collaboratively in group contexts	### Speaking and listening Ask the children to experiment with the names of those in their group to create an alliterative sentence. Tell them that the sentence does not need to make absolute sense.	**Support:** use dictionaries to find suitable alliterations
	### Independent work Encourage the children to write their alliterative sentence on a sheet of paper, using large clear writing.	
	### Plenary Let each group stand in front of the class, holding up their strips of paper. The class should read the sentences aloud. Discuss any tongue-twisting effects.	

DAY 2 ◾ Nursery rhymes

Key features	Stages	Additional opportunities
Reasoning: explain their opinion about poems, using words and phrases to support their ideas	### Introduction Ask the children what nursery rhymes they know, and if they know them by heart. Invite the children to recite some nursery rhymes or recite some for them. Display *Little Miss Muffet, Georgie Porgie* and *Hickory, Dickory, Dock* from the CD-ROM. Tell the children to read the rhymes one by one and say what is unusual about them. Explain that the writer has used well-known, familiar rhymes as a basis for writing new ones. Encourage the children to suggest what effect he wanted to achieve. Ask the children to recite the original versions and compare them. Ask them to say which are the funniest. Recite *Sing a song of sixpence* from photocopiable page 191 'Silly rhymes' to the children. Write the opening few words of each line on the board and collaborate with the class to add new endings for each line to create a funny or silly effect.	
Creative thinking: respond imaginatively	### Speaking and listening Ask the children to work with a partner and to think of a sillier version of the rhyme to use as part of a class poem.	**Support:** use photocopiable page 191 'Silly rhymes' to rewrite the rhyme **Extend:** use photocopiable page 192 'Incy Wincy Spider'
Evaluation: review written work against agreed criteria	### Plenary Encourage the children to feed back their ideas to the class to produce a collaborative class poem. Discuss and compare the effects of the children's different ideas. Ask the children to say which ones they think are the funniest. Discuss the children's writing so far in this Unit. Tell them to evaluate their successes and say where they think they need to improve.	

Guided reading

Provide other sorts of humorous poetry for the group at an appropriate level, for example limericks, and nonsense poetry by Edward Lear. Ask the children to identify words used to create humour and impact.

Assessment

Self assessment: Ask the children what they need to do to improve their writing.

Observation: Do the children recognise invented words?

Do they recognise how rhyme, and rhythm affect the way poems are read?

Refer back to the learning outcomes on page 183.

Further work

Ask the children to invent new words to describe sounds and movements.

Ask the children to clap the beats of poems as they read them aloud.

DAY 1 ◼ Rainbow

Key features	Stages	Additional opportunities
Reasoning: explain their opinion about poems, using words and phrases to support their ideas	### Introduction Display the poem *Rainbow* from the CD-ROM with the title hidden and read it to the class. Ask the children to say what they think is being described and find the evidence in the poem. Discuss any vocabulary the children might not understand, such as *indigo, wold* and *crock*. Ask the children to identify the rhyming words. Annotate the text to show how different pairs of sequential lines rhyme and the last three lines. Read it together, emphasising or clapping the rhythm. Ask the children to look carefully at each line and say if they notice anything unusual about the way this poem is written. Elicit that the initial letters of the lines spell rainbow when read vertically. Explain that this is an acrostic poem. ### Speaking and listening Tell the children to work in groups and brainstorm ideas for writing an acrostic poem. ### Independent work Ask the children to work in pairs, to choose an idea for an acrostic poem and begin writing a draft together. ### Plenary Remind the children of the different types of poetry they have been reading in this Unit. Ask them to suggest what they have in common. Elicit that they all use language in unusual ways. Ask them to say which they prefer and give reasons for their opinions. Let some of the groups feed back the ideas for acrostic poems from the brainstorming session.	**Support:** use *Poetry* from the CD-ROM

DAY 2 ◼ Acrostic poems

Key features	Stages	Additional opportunities
Creative thinking: respond imaginatively to a stimulus	### Introduction Explain to the children that they are going to write their paired acrostic poems in this session on screen. Choose one of the children's ideas from the previous session and write down the images associated with it. Explain that you want to include some of them in your poem and that you are not going to make this poem rhyme but you want it to have a strong rhythm. Ask the children for some suggestions and model writing them on the board, changing words and word order to create a rhythmic effect. Using slideshow software, model how to write the word in capital letters in a vertical line. Add new lines using new screens to build up to a cumulative final screen of the complete poem or, using one screen, reveal the lines one by one of the complete poem. ### Independent work Ask the pairs of children to complete the draft acrostic poems began in the previous session. They should them write them on screen using slideshow software. ### Plenary View all the children's poems. Discuss which ones are most effective and why. The poems could be shared with other classes via the school website or via email to children at another school.	**Support:** write their whole poem on one screen only **Extend:** can use special effects to reveal lines of the poem one at a time

Guided writing

Work with groups as they write their acrostic poems. Identify where they could add poetic language, alliteration and similes.

Assessment

Self assessment: Children evaluate their progress against agreed success criteria and their personal targets.
Observation: Are the children able to change vocabulary and re-order words in their lines of poetry to create a rhythmical effect?
Children complete the interactive CD-ROM assessment activity 'Snowdrop'.
Refer back to the learning outcomes on page 183.

Further work

Ask the children to use colour and font effects on the computer to emphasise the initial letters of each line of their acrostic poems.

To rhyme or not to rhyme

■ Choose words to end each pair of lines so that they rhyme.

■ Then choose again so they do not rhyme.

Writing Poetry

I wrote one verse and then another.

I tried to read them to my ———————————

He didn't like it much at all

And went outside to play ———————————

I tried to read them to my friend

Who didn't like the way they ———————————

My teacher said they ought to rhyme

But doing that takes too much ———————————

Instead I think I'll write a play

But do it on another ———————————

Writing Poetry

I wrote one verse and then another.

I tried to read them to my ———————————

He didn't like it much at all

And went outside to play ———————————

I tried to read them to my friend

Who didn't like the way they ———————————

My teacher said they ought to rhyme

But doing that takes too much ———————————

Instead I think I'll write a play

But do it on another ———————————

■ 100 LITERACY FRAMEWORK LESSONS YEAR 3

Name _____ Date _____

Silly rhymes

■ Choose words from the bottom of the page to make a funny nursery rhyme.

Sing a song of sixpence
A pocket full of rye.
Four and twenty blackbirds
baked in a pie.
When the pie was opened
The birds began to sing.
Wasn't that a dainty dish
To set before the King.

Sing a song of _____

A pocket full of rye.

Four and twenty _____

Baked in a pie.

When the pie was _____

The _____ began to sing

Wasn't that a _____ dish

To set before the King.

dumplings	piglets	eaten	singing
sizzling	silly	dopey	tasty
butterflies	flutter	crazy	sausages

Name _____   Date _____

Incy Wincy Spider

■ Fill in the gaps to make a new rhyme.

Incy Wincy Spider climbed up _____

Down came _____

Which made the spider _____

Up _____

And _____

So _____

■ 100 LITERACY FRAMEWORK LESSONS YEAR 3